Lincoln's Religion

Lincoln's Religion

William J. Wolf

PILGRIM PRESS

Philadelphia   Boston

Library of Congress Catalog Card Number 70-123035
SBN 8298-0181-2

United Church Press
Philadelphia, Pennsylvania

The first edition, published in 1959 by Doubleday & Company, Inc., carried the title *The Almost Chosen People*. A revised edition, published in 1963 by The Seabury Press, was entitled *The Religion of Abraham Lincoln*.

"The Creed of Abraham Lincoln in His Own Words" is from *The Soul of Abraham Lincoln* by William E. Barton. Copyright 1920 by William E. Barton. Reprinted by permission of Bruce Barton.

To my wife ELEANOR
and to our boys
EDWIN, JOHN, and STEPHEN

Preface to Paperback Edition

Lincoln's Religion is the paperback version of the book that first appeared in 1959 as *The Almost Chosen People* and again in 1963 in a revised edition with another publisher as *The Religion of Abraham Lincoln*. My third publisher now insists on the title *Lincoln's Religion*. Friends and reviewers chided me for the confusion before. What they will now say I can well imagine. My solace is seeing the book back in print. My embarrassment at three titles is well described in a story Lincoln told Senator Henderson as he watched three of his congressional critics crossing the White House lawn to put pressure on him.

"I attended . . . school . . . in Indiana where we had no reading books or grammars, and all our reading was done from the Bible. We stood in a long line and read in turn from it. One day our lesson was the story of the three Hebrew children and their escape from the fiery furnace.

It fell to a little towheaded fellow who stood next to me to read for the first time the verse with the unpronounceable names. He made a sorry mess of Shadrach and Meshach, and went all to pieces on Abednego. Whereupon the master boxed his ears until he sobbed aloud. Then the lesson went on, each boy in the class reading a verse in turn. Finally the towheaded boy stopped crying, but only to fix his gaze upon the verses ahead, and set up a yell of surprise and alarm. The master demanded the reason for this unexpected outbreak. 'Look there, master,' said the boy, pointing his finger at the verse which in a few moments he would be expected to read, and at the three proper names which it contained, 'there comes them same damn three fellows again!' "

In the tangled forest of conflicting statements about Lincoln's religion or his lack of it, there are many pitfalls for the unwary. Until Lincoln's own speeches and writings were established by the publication, in 1953, of the definitive nine-volume *Collected Works of Abraham Lincoln* under the editorship of Roy Basler, a writer on Lincoln's religion could not proceed to his task without losing momentum arguing for or against the authenticity of a given letter or text. Now it is possible to accept this core of confirmed Lincoln utterance and to let Lincoln illuminate his own religion by his own words. That is the method followed in this study. It then becomes possible, with Lincoln's own statements as the norm, to sift with caution

8

those of some of his contemporaries about his religion, especially those about his early years. Lincoln won his way to ever deeper levels of faith in response to family suffering and national tragedy. His religion was not static, but dynamic in its development.

So many letters have come from people sincerely convinced that Lincoln was a member of their particular denomination or about to become such that a special appendix has been added on this point.

Some recent bibliographical references have been added. No letters or papers of Lincoln have been discovered in the last few years that would lead me to revise the earlier characterization of Lincoln as a "biblical prophet" who saw himself as "an instrument of God" and his country as God's "almost chosen people" called to domestic and world responsibility. How we as a nation conceive and act our role in the light of Lincoln's deliberately ambiguous qualifier "almost" may determine our destiny in the years ahead.

The author's indebtedness to Lincoln scholars is too great to acknowledge in detail. I am particularly grateful to Dr. David Mearns, of the Library of Congress, for his encouragement and help.

Contents

11

13

Lincoln's Religion

"I Made a Solemn Vow before God"

Chapter 1

It was September 22, 1862. The President's Cabinet was in session to consider an urgent problem on which Lincoln wanted advice. Secretary of the Treasury Salmon Chase had just asked the President to repeat what he had been saying. Lincoln had described his decision to emancipate the slaves in territories then in rebellion against the federal government. Toward the end the President's voice had become lower and more solemn. Secretary Chase wanted to be certain he had understood Lincoln's words. The President repeated:

"I made a solemn vow before God, that if General Lee was driven back from Pennsylvania, I would crown the result by the declaration of freedom to the slaves."[1]

At times writers have not reported this incident in their accounts of the cabinet session. Many omit the specific statement of Lincoln about a "solemn vow before God" and describe instead "a solemn resolution." This, however, is to substitute a black and white photograph with blurred focus for the rich colors of a masterpiece. The problem is not one of historical evidence. Few incidents in Lincoln's life are so well documented as this one. The quotation used is from the artist Francis Carpenter, who lived in the White House at the President's invitation as he worked on his painting of the reading of the Proclamation. Carpenter interviewed all who were present at the event and has recorded the most minute particulars in his famous book published in 1866. Had they found any inaccuracy the members of the Cabinet might have challenged him at this early date.

In addition to Carpenter's careful records there are at least two accounts from the diaries of cabinet members. The first is the statement of Secretary Chase:

"The President then took a graver tone, and said, Gentlemen: I have, as you are aware, thought a great deal about the relation of this war to slavery; and you all remember that, several weeks ago, I read to you an order I had prepared on this subject, which, on account of objections made by some of you, was not issued. Ever since then my mind has been much occupied with this subject, and I have thought, all along, that the time for acting on it might probably come. I think the time has come now. I wish it were a better time. I wish that we were in a better condition. The action of the army against the rebels has not been quite what I should best like. But they have been driven out of Maryland, and Pennsylvania is no longer in danger of invasion. When the Rebel Army was at Frederick, I determined, as soon as it should be driven out of Maryland, to issue a Proclamation of Emancipation, such as I thought most likely to be useful. I said nothing to anyone, but I made a promise to myself, and (hesitating a little) to my Maker. The Rebel Army is now driven out, and I am going to fulfill that promise."[2]

The second confirmation comes from the diary of Gideon Welles, the Secretary of the Navy:

"We have a special Cabinet meeting. The subject was the Proclamation concerning emancipating slaves. . . . There were some differences in the Cabinet, but he had formed his own conclusions, and made his own decisions. He had, he said, made a vow, a covenant, that if God gave us the victory in the approaching battle (which had just been fought) he would consider it his duty to move forward in the cause of emancipation. We might think it strange, he said, but there were times when he felt uncertain how to act; that he had in this way submitted the disposal of matters when the way was not clear to his mind what he should do. God had decided this question in favor of the slave. He was satisfied it was right—was confirmed and strengthened by the vow and its results; his mind was fixed, his decision made; but he wished his paper announcing his course to be as correct in terms as it could be made without any attempt to change his determination. For that was fixed."[3]

The testimony is incontrovertible. Lincoln reached his decision about the timing of the Proclamation in an immediate awareness of the presence of God. For Lincoln, God was not a "cosmic blur," nor the parsons' "stock in trade," nor the politicians' benediction over spread-eagle oratory. God was ultimate yet personal reality, and He made Himself accessible to one who sought Him out. For Lincoln, God was the final court of appeal when he was uncertain about the moral aspects of a question. God's guidance was sought when Lincoln wanted to pass through the tides of political expediency to stand on bedrock.

One is prompted to ask why in traditional accounts of this cabinet session many historians have omitted the very key to understanding it. They would probably reply that their task is to show the sociological, political, and economic factors in the evolution of Lincoln's attitude toward emancipation. Their studies are of course tremendously valuable in just this area. They bring a needed corrective to the mythological picture of the young flatboater in New Orleans vowing to crush "that thing" and there and then charting a course toward the White House with abolitionist banner flying.

We can better understand Lincoln's final act of emancipation when we realize that for long he was balked by a dilemma. He believed that despite the moral wrong of slavery the federal government was prevented by the Constitution from disturbing it in the original states. He had early accepted the Missouri Compromise as a practical way of getting along between North and South. It was the upsetting of this balance by the passage of the Kansas-Nebraska Act that drew Lincoln again into the political arena. He felt called to oppose Douglas's doctrine of "popular sovereignty" by which territories would themselves determine whether to enter the federal Union as slave or as free states. In his early years as President, Lincoln held off the abolitionists with his argument that he was sworn to defend the Union. Only, it seemed, as an act of military necessity could he free the slaves in the conviction that a technically unconstitutional step might be needed to preserve the Union itself.

The sequence of events just before Lincoln's decision is interesting. Horace Greeley attempted to dictate to Lincoln in an open letter in the *Tribune* entitled "The Prayer of Twenty Millions" and demanded immediate emancipation. Lincoln stated his position with forceful clarity in a letter to the editor on August 22, 1862.

"My paramount object in this struggle *is* to save the Union, and is *not* either to save or to destroy slavery. If I could save the Union without freeing *any* slave I would do it, and if I could save it by freeing *all* the slaves I would do it; and if I could save it by freeing some and leaving others alone, I would also do that. What I do about slavery, and the colored race, I do because I believe it helps to save the Union; and what I forbear, I forbear because I do *not* believe it would help to save the Union. I shall do *less* whenever I shall believe what I am doing hurts the cause, and I shall do *more* whenever I shall believe doing more will help the cause. I shall try to correct errors when shown to be errors; and I shall adopt new views so fast as they shall appear to be true views.

"I have here stated my purpose according to my view of *official* duty; and I intend no modification of my oft-expressed *personal* wish that all men everywhere could be free."[4]

Three weeks later he was waited upon by two clergymen who presented a memorial from a mass meeting of Chicago Christians of all denominations. He listened to the document, which demanded immediate emancipation, and then replied with a firmness probably stiffened by his distaste for the oversimplification of a very complex issue:

"I am approached with the most opposite opinions and advice, and that by religious men, who are equally certain that they represent the divine will. I am sure that either the one or the other class is mistaken in that belief, and perhaps in some respects both. I hope it will not be irreverent for me to say that if it is probable that God would reveal his will to others, on a point so connected with my duty, it might be supposed he would reveal it directly to me; for, unless I am more deceived in myself than I often am, it is my earnest desire to know the will of Providence in this matter. *And if I can learn what it is, I will do it!* These are not, however, the days of miracles, and I suppose it will be granted that I am not to expect a direct revelation. I must study the plain, physical facts of the case, ascertain what is possible and learn what appears to be wise and right. The subject is difficult, and good men do not agree."

He then spoke of division in a New York delegation that had been to see him and of perplexity in the last Congress, even though the majority were anti-slavery. He pointedly went on:

"Why, the rebel soldiers are praying with a great deal more earnestness, I fear, than our own troops, and expecting God to favor their side; for one of our soldiers, who had been taken prisoner, told Senator Wilson, a few days since, that he met with nothing so discouraging as the evident sincerity of those he was among in their prayers."

Lincoln then analyzed the pros and cons of the proposal and invited a reply. The two clergymen replied point by point in an hour of earnest discussion. The interview ended with the President saying:

"Do not misunderstand me, because I have mentioned these objections. They indicate the difficulties that have thus far prevented my action in some such way as you desire. I have not decided against a proclamation of liberty to the slaves, but hold the matter under advisement. And I can assure you that the subject is on my mind, by day and night, more than any other. Whatever shall appear to be God's will I will do. I trust that, in the freedom with which I have canvassed your views, I have not in any respect injured your feelings."[5]

At the end of the week following the visit of the Chicago delegation Lincoln summoned his Cabinet. He was ready to issue a proclamation freeing most of the slaves, but first, heeding Seward's earlier advice, he had wanted a victory such as Antietam. He did not want the act to be interpreted as the despairing gesture of a sorely pressed government. Also he had been seeking to submit this question to higher authority, to the God Who, he firmly believed, presided over man's history and Who acted within that history, even if His will might be difficult for man to understand. By the date of the cabinet session Lincoln was convinced that "God had decided this question in favor of the slave. He was satisfied it was right—was confirmed and strengthened by the vow and its results."

Clearly Lincoln's motivation in this historic act had much more to it than politics or military necessity. His decision was not made "apart" from these factors, in a vacuum of the soul, but "beyond" them. This "transhistorical" dimension in Lincoln illuminates the course of history itself. Historians by their conventional methods describe events as a chemist might analyze the pigmentation on a masterpiece. It was given to Lincoln, however, in a uniquely imaginative way to stand at the perspective from which the divine artist paints his canvas and to help others to appreciate that masterpiece.

In this sense Lincoln is one of the greatest theologians of America—not in the technical meaning of producing a system of doctrine, certainly not as the defender of some one denomination, but in the sense of seeing the hand of God intimately in the affairs of nations. Just so the prophets of Israel criticized the events of their day from the perspective of the God Who is concerned for history and Who reveals His will within it. Lincoln stands among God's latter-day prophets.

Although many Christians in his time tried to describe God's judgments in history they usually produced a wooden and unconvincing oversimplification. It ministered to the self-righteousness of the one making the judgment. An obvious case in point was the doctrinaire theory of the abolitionists that every evil in America stemmed from Southern slaveholders. Lincoln saw the complexity of historical processes, the mixture of human motivations, and man's incurable self-righteousness. All three bedevil human history. For Lincoln, God's judgments were enacted organically within history rather than forced upon it mechanically from without.

This can best be illustrated by his view of the moral question in slavery, which became ever clearer to him after his debates with Douglas. The country was founded upon the belief expressed in the Declaration of Independence that all men were created equal. Slavery was a living lie in contradicting that fundamental principle which for Lincoln had the force of divine revelation. The Civil War he came to understand as the punishment visited by God upon a nation denying its true destiny by its refusal to put slavery "in process of ultimate extinction." The war came as the final organic breakdown within the nation of this built-in contradiction to the law of its life. Lincoln would never have denied the political, psychological, and economic causes of the Civil War. Indeed, he could articulate them sharply, but he pressed beyond them to see the whole sweep of the nation's history in terms of God's judgments and mercies. Lincoln saw American history in the freshness of prophetic insight. He is the American Isaiah, or Jeremiah, or St. Paul.

This book will attempt to explore this "transhistorical" dimension in Lincoln and to show how it complements rather than negates the important historical studies of recent years. It will try to show how Lincoln's living awareness of God helped him resolve his ethical dilemmas ("there were times when he felt uncertain how to act") and take responsible action "with firmness in the right, as God gives us to see the right" and yet "with charity for all."

It would be unfair, however, to reproach careful historians for not giving us all the story behind the Proclamation of Emancipation, if one did not offer some justification for their shying away from the religious dimension in Lincoln. There developed immediately after his death a religion about Lincoln as "the dying God." This cult has been scrutinized provocatively by Lloyd Lewis in *Myths after Lincoln*. The mythologized picture was soon read back into the day-to-day events of his life to the utter confusion of the historical record. Against this tissue of legend the critical historians of Lincoln have rightly protested.

Many members of the Christian community, moreover, have added to the confusion. They have been shameless in claiming Lincoln as a secret member of their denomination or about to become such. Many parsons sought publicity and self-glorification in their accounts of supposed conversations with Lincoln. Others, like Father Chiniquy, who did have interviews put the most improbable speeches into Lincoln's mouth. The conflicting evidence on Lincoln's religion is incredibly complex. One could "prove" about anything by selecting what he wanted from the sources. The fair-minded investigator must finally admit that the only really reliable testimony, with a few exceptions, must be gleaned from Lincoln's own speeches and letters. This central core of authentic Lincoln utterance in the Rutgers edition of his works must be the acid test for other supplementary evidence critically evaluated.

An example of the caution that must be exercised is provided by the famous "Beecher incident," which snowballed from nothing into a pious tale widely circulated by uncritical writers. Dr. Chapman accepted its authenticity in his *Latest Light on Lincoln,* claiming that "upon the scene of this unique event there rests a halo of celestial beauty too sacred to be regarded with indifference or doubt."

According to a grandson of Henry Ward Beecher who claimed to have heard it from Mrs. Beecher "in her old age," Lincoln after the disaster of Bull Run appeared at their Brooklyn door with his face hidden in a military cloak. Without giving his name he asked to see the famous preacher. The anxious Mrs. Beecher at her husband's bidding admitted the suspicious character. Behind closed doors she heard their voices and the pacing of their feet until the mysterious visitor left about midnight. Shortly before Beecher's death he is supposed to have revealed that his caller was Lincoln in disguise.

"Alone for hours that night, like Jacob of old, the two had wrestled together in prayer with the God of battles and the Watcher over the right until they had received the help which He had promised to those that seek His aid."[6]

While it is unthinkable that the President would have stolen away secretly from Washington at a time of national crisis when he might just as well have summoned Beecher to Washington if he wanted to see him, the story still has its defenders. The really decisive evidence against it was provided by Beecher himself. Along with others, he was asked to contribute reminiscences of Lincoln to the *North American Review*. He never described anything remotely resembling this Nicodemus visit and said he really did not know Lincoln very well personally!

Even highly respected members of the Christian community have fallen into serious error by accepting the accounts of others in good faith but with historical naïveté. There is a famous example of this with respect to the cabinet meeting under discussion. Bishop Charles Henry Fowler devoted some one hundred pages to Lincoln in his *Patriotic Orations*, published in 1910. The speech had its origin in a funeral eulogy delivered in Chicago on May 4, 1865, and was repeated by popular request hundreds of times over more than thirty years.

Bishop Fowler had heard that at the beginning of the cabinet meeting Lincoln read from a book. What book could it be? Either Bishop Fowler caught the suggestion from another pious source or he supplied what he thought was the appropriate book for such a momentous occasion. Bishop Fowler said he read a chapter from the Bible. Secretary Chase wrote that he read a chapter from the humorist Artemus Ward on "A High-Handed Outrage at Utica."

What is plainly needed in the exploration of Lincoln's religion is the historian's rigorous rejection of the mythologized picture and yet an honest wrestling with the irreducible religious core that illuminates his acts. It may even be that Lincoln's humor throws some light upon his religious faith. This would not have been understood by the humorless and pompous Chase, who reported of the cabinet session: ". . . [Lincoln] proposed to read a chapter which he thought very funny. Read it, and seemed to enjoy it very much."

There is still another problem about Lincoln's religion that has been a source of embarrassment to many people. They are worried about anyone taking such a vow as Lincoln made. They object that this reduces man's relationship to God to a transactional level. ("I'll free the slaves if You, God, will give us victory.") They argue that it savors of primitive superstition and has no place in a reasoned faith. Both dangers are obviously serious ones and could prove fatal in the hands of a fanatic or even of a lesser man. The element that rescues Lincoln is the integrity of his vision of God's will and his unself-righteous perspective on himself. Lincoln's view of reality had, however, an element of the primitive in it represented by the vow and also by his interest in dreams as foretelling the future.

Lamon has recorded the dream that came to Lincoln shortly before his death and claims that his recollection of Lincoln's words was based on notes taken just after the event. Lincoln dreamed that he heard invisible mourners in the White House. He explored until in the East Room he saw a catafalque with a corpse guarded by soldiers. "Who is dead in the White House?" he demanded of one. "The President," came the reply; "he was killed by an assassin!" Turning to Mrs. Lincoln, Lamon, and the others present, Lincoln added:

"It seems strange how much there is in the Bible about dreams. There are, I think, some sixteen chapters in the Old Testament and four or five in the New in which dreams are mentioned . . . If we believe the Bible, we must accept the fact that in the old days God and His angels came to men in their sleep and made themselves known in dreams. Nowadays dreams are regarded as very foolish, and are seldom told, except by old women and by young men and maidens in love. . . . After it occurred, the first time I opened the Bible, strange as it may appear, it was at the twenty-eighth chapter of Genesis, which related the wonderful dream Jacob had. I turned to other passages, and seemed to encounter a dream or a vision wherever I looked. I kept on turning the leaves of the old book, and everywhere my eye fell upon passages recording matters strangely in keeping with my own thoughts,—supernatural visitations, dreams, visions, etc."[7]

This resort to a vow, the concern about dreams, and some inquiries into spiritualism were survivals of the primitive biblicism and backwoods superstition that characterized frontier religion. While this influence was undoubtedly strong on Lincoln, there is the opposite side of him with its highly rational criticism of popular religion. In the incident with which we began this chapter it is important to note Lincoln's words that the vow "confirmed and strengthened" *his own decision*. It did not magically replace that careful weighing of evidence and logical analysis which is so characteristically a part of his perennial appeal. This side of his nature he expressed to the Chicago clergymen: "I suppose . . . I am not to expect a direct revelation. I must study the plain, physical facts of the case, ascertain what is possible and learn what appears to be wise and right."

It is clear that Lincoln's religion had many facets. Only caricature can result from seizing upon one element within the complex and neglecting to evaluate other significant and modifying factors. The simplest description of his religion would be "singlehearted integrity in humbly seeking to understand God's will in the affairs of men and his own responsibility therein." The development of that religion and its expression in his life will be the subject of this study. Lincoln's simplicity of purpose and his religious awareness have been movingly expressed by Stephen Vincent Benét in a poetic paraphrase of Lincoln's own words.

What is God's will?

They come to me and talk about God's will
In righteous deputations and platoons,
Day after day, laymen and ministers.
They write me Prayers From Twenty Million Souls
Defining me God's will and Horace Greeley's.
God's will is General This and Senator That,
God's will is those poor colored fellows' will,

It is the will of the Chicago churches,
It is this man's and his worst enemy's.
But all of them are sure they know God's will.
I am the only man who does not know it.

And, yet, if it is probable that God
Should, and so very clearly, state His will
To others on a point of my own duty,
It might be thought He would reveal it me
Directly, more especially as I
So earnestly desire to know His will.[8]

Chapter 2

Abraham Lincoln
his hand and pen.
he will be good but
god knows When.[1]

These lines are the first selection in the eight-volume Rutgers
edition of Lincoln's *Collected Works*. They were written in an
arithmetic book Lincoln put together for himself. A typical piece
of schoolboy doggerel, it probably was not composed by him.
It is amusing to see what some writers of the pious school have
done with this ditty. Dr. Chapman wrote: "It is profoundly
significant that this child of destiny, at his life's early morning,
in clumsy but impressive verse thus reverently coupled his
name with that of his Creator."[2] If one searched long enough

in the tangled jungle of the debate over Lincoln's religion one could probably find a representative of the skeptical school using these lines as proof positive of a dawning atheism, considering that "god" is not capitalized.

It is not in supposedly clairvoyant statements of his childhood that we are to anticipate the faith of his mature years, for with few exceptions Lincoln was reticent about discussing his religion directly. If we are to find shadows of coming events in his early years they must be in terms of his home environment and the frontier religion of the regions in which the Lincolns settled.

Research into Lincoln genealogy has established some facts that would have interested Lincoln. He admits in one of his autobiographical sketches that he could not learn much about his ancestors. His progenitor, Samuel Lincoln, came to the Massachusetts Bay Colony in 1637. He is reported to have helped in the building of the Old Ship Church in Hingham, claimed today to be the oldest church building in America in continual use. Mordecai Lincoln II, his great-great-grand-father, married a granddaughter of Abadiah Holmes, a Newport Baptist who was flogged on Boston Common for his dissenting opinions and practice. Lincolns who emigrated to the Shenandoah Valley of Virginia were also Baptists. Lincoln's grandfather Abraham donated a piece of his four-hundred-acre tract near Louisville, Kentucky, on which the Long Run Baptist Church was built. Here in its graveyard he lies, shot by an Indian while at work in his cornfield.

Although Lincoln's parents, Thomas and Nancy, were married by Jesse Head, a Methodist circuit rider, they appear to have become members of the Little Mount Separate Baptist

Church. The anti-slavery position of this Little Mount Church may throw some light on Lincoln's statement that his father left Kentucky "partly on account of slavery" and that he could not remember a time when he himself did not think slavery was wrong.

The Separate Baptists in Kentucky were distinguished from Regular Baptists in that they accepted no creed save the Bible itself while the latter group stood on the Philadelphia Confession of Faith. According to the custom of the times, young Abraham was probably carried horseback in his mother's arms when the family went to meeting.

In 1816 the Lincolns removed from the hilly limestone farms of Kentucky to the heavily wooded area of southern Indiana. Later Lincoln described their situation in verse:

> When first my father settled here,
> 'Twas then the frontier line;
> The panther's scream filled night with fear
> And bears preyed on the swine.[3]

Less poetically, his mother's cousin Dennis Hanks said, "We lived the same as the Indians, 'ceptin' we took an interest in politics and religion."

In their early Indiana years the family was cut off from much contact with itinerating parsons. The Bible was probably the only book this frontier family owned. Lincoln is said to have told a friend, "My mother was a ready reader and read the Bible to me habitually." Some Lincoln scholars maintain, however, that Nancy Hanks was illiterate. He learned by heart some of the biblical texts which his mother sang as she worked at chores in the cabin. One of the campaign biographies for which Lincoln furnished material describes mother, son, and daughter taking turns reading the Scriptures on the Sabbath. Their family Bible had been published in 1799 by the Society for the Propagation of Christian Knowledge. In addition to the text it had "arguments prefixed to the different books and moral and theological observations illustrating each chapter, composed by the Reverend Mr. Ostervald, Professor of Divinity." This was the battered old Bible from which Lincoln was seen reading in the White House.

When Abraham was nine years old death came to their Indiana cabin. Nancy Hanks died in an epidemic of the "milk sick." Her husband whipsawed rough boards into a respectable coffin and buried Nancy on a little knoll not far from the cabin as the autumn leaves were beginning to drop. The boy questioned why God had taken his mother away when he so desperately needed her. He searched but found no answer. After a time Parson David Elkin, whom the Lincolns had known at the Little Mount Church in Kentucky, visited them. In the forest clearing near Gentryville the minister conducted a memorial service for the pioneer mother, speaking words of Christian hope.

The traditional picture of the father Thomas as "shiftless" has been corrected by modern research. Within a year of Nancy's death he returned to Elizabethtown and induced Sarah Bush Johnston to become his second wife. In Indiana he helped establish the Pigeon Creek Baptist Church and became a leading member of the congregation. He served as moderator, trustee, and reconciler in matters of church discipline. He contributed to its upkeep.

It is difficult to establish the particular brand of Baptist beliefs that characterized this congregation. Lincoln's stepmother's statement to Herndon might be interpreted to mean that it was more liberal than the "hard-shell" variety. The evidence, however, in the Deerskin record book points toward "hard-shell" doctrine. Its dominant theological position was predestination, the belief that God had foreordained all events by divine decree from eternity. Its corollary was that only those predestinated would be saved. Sandburg pictures the boy Lincoln puzzling over that long word "predestination." Other characteristic features were foot washing, rejection of a paid and educated ministry, and opposition to musical instruments in worship. There was also among "hard-shells" resistance to missionary activity in foreign lands, and to such newfangled notions as Sunday schools for unregenerate children.

For some reason, possibly because of differences between "Separate" and "Regular" Baptists, Thomas Lincoln was not received as a member of the Pigeon Creek church by letter of transfer until June 7, 1823. Sister Lincoln was received the same day "by experience." Abraham's sister Sally was admitted to membership on April 8, 1826. It was of course an adult congregation with a membership that was mainly married. Sally's joining preceded her marriage to Aaron Grigsby by about four months. Abraham never joined, perhaps because he was not yet ready to marry and settle down or perhaps for reservations which he was keeping to himself. A visitor to the Pigeon Creek church in 1866 reported finding in the loft a record book with the entry "1 broom, ½ dozen tallow candles" and signed "Abe Lincoln, Sexton."

We know that he enjoyed mimicking these hell-fire and brimstone preachers who shouted and flailed the air as if "they were fighting bees." Ward Hill Lamon, whose account of the Hoosier years was based on reminiscences of old-time residents of Spencer County, described this spirited imitation. "On Monday mornings he would mount a stump, and deliver, with a wonderful approach to exactness, the sermon he had heard the day before. . . . His step sister, Matilda Johnston, says he was an indefatigable 'preacher.' When father and mother would go to church, Abe would take down the Bible, read a verse, give out a hymn, and we would sing. Abe was about fifteen years of age. He preached, and we would do the crying. Sometimes he would join in the chorus of tears."[4] This frontier preaching was a country lad's first introduction to public speaking and he lapped it up.

His simple, God-fearing parents were accustomed to say grace at meals. A visitor reported that Thomas' usual words were: "Fit and prepare us for Life's humblest service, for Christ's sake. Amen." Once the boy spoke up when the meal consisted of nothing but potatoes, "Dad, I call these mighty poor blessings."

Testimony from his relatives is conflicting about his own study of Scripture, but at some time and in some manner he acquired a profound knowledge of its contents. The proof of this is apparent from his later speeches and from the interest he displayed when President in tracking down special texts.

Lincoln's knowledge of the Bible far exceeded the content-grasp of most present-day clergymen.

Direct evidence for his acquaintance with the Bible at this period of his life can be found in his parody of biblical narration. *The Chronicles of Reuben* were written shortly before his first trip to New Orleans. This bit of buffoonery resulted from hard feeling between Lincoln and the Grigsby brothers. When two Grigsby brothers married sisters on the same day Lincoln took part in a plot which sent the young husbands into the bedrooms of the wrong brides. The trick was discovered in time, but it naturally created no little turmoil.

The raw lad committed a further indiscretion by putting the episode into writing as *The Chronicles of Reuben* in the heroic manner of the patriarchal narratives. Thus clumsily he showed a feeling for style in writing. The backwoods parson gave him his first picture of the public speaker and the imitation of the Bible provided his first faltering attempt at composition. Frontier religion was the vehicle of culture for this Hoosier youth as it was the chief civilizing influence in its region.

Lincoln helped his family pack up its belongings and move on into Illinois prairie country in 1830. He stayed with them until a cabin was constructed and a fair beginning made for planting. Then, having come of age, he left them to go off on his own. Neither farming nor carpentry appealed to him. His relations with his father may well have been strained. Lincoln's love of reading must have seemed to Thomas a useless luxury in the hard struggle to keep alive. One speculates as to whether the father may have justified his own ignorance on religious grounds and so proved a stumbling block to a son eager to learn more about his world. The frontier parsons he had met up to this time boasted that they had never attended college or seminary, which they looked upon as centers of devilish infidelity. For many of them a lack of education was next to Godliness.

The word "infidel" was freely and loosely used. A person who held that the earth traveled around the sun would be an "infidel." Anyone who had doubts about the Bible would be an "infidel." A Christian of another denomination was occasionally labeled an "infidel." The tactic of backwoods religion in meeting skeptical criticism was to shout it down as a work of the devil. There was no disposition to meet it on the level of debate, using the scientific understanding of the day to convince the skeptic. It would be a new experience for Lincoln to come to know in Springfield churches having settled pastors who were college-trained and who sought to reconcile the Bible with current historical and scientific knowledge.

"A piece of floating driftwood" was Lincoln's description of himself when he moved to New Salem in 1831 as the enterprising protégé of Denton Offutt, a small-town promoter. Offutt had been impressed with Lincoln's ingenuity in getting his flatboat over the dam at New Salem. He set Lincoln up to tend a store and a mill he had bought in this growing community of about twenty-five families.

There was no church building in New Salem, but the Rev. John M. Berry, one of the settlers, held services in his or neighboring houses. A leader of culture in the community, he removed to Iowa in 1849 and published there a book entitled *Lectures on the Covenants and Right to Church Membership.*

Berry was a Presbyterian as was Dr. Allen, a Yankee from Vermont and Dartmouth College, somewhat out of place in this Southern pioneer atmosphere. Allen gave his New England conscience scope, however, by founding a temperance society and by organizing the first Sunday school in New Salem. Mentor Graham, Lincoln's tutor, and a local schoolmaster, was a leading Baptist.

The Methodists turned out in yearly revivals. These camp meetings were often conducted by the roving, colorful Peter Cartwright. "Uncle Peter," as he was affectionately called, reports in his autobiography that at one of his services five hundred people started "jerking" at once. Women were particularly susceptible to this revivalistic enthusiasm. As their caps and combs came loose, Onstot, a local resident, reported, "so sudden would be the jerking of the head that their long loose hair would crack almost as loud as a waggoner's whip."

The crude emotionalism of these gatherings can hardly have commended itself to Lincoln with his strong sense of humor and of reserve in matters of the spirit. What must have disturbed him still more was the violent feuding between the jealous denominations. One form of Baptist predestinarian opinion held that its church members were created by God for heaven whereas the greater part of mankind had been destined for eternal flames. Methodist and Baptist denounced each other on whether the road to heaven passed over dry land or water. Local roughs tossed logs into the Sangamon River when baptisms were scheduled.

Some perspective on this loveless sectarianism was given by a Yale graduate who came to teach. "In Illinois," he wrote,

"I met for the first time a divided Christian community and was plunged without warning and preparation into a sea of sectarian rivalries, which was kept in constant agitation."

In his fascinating picture of the New Salem community Benjamin Thomas summarized Lincoln's reactions to his religious environment: "He entered with zest into the theological discussions of the community, and profited by the niceties of thought, the subtle distinctions and the fine spun argument that they necessitated. Yet, while he enjoyed them as a mental exercise, and while he eventually attained to a deep faith, emotionally the bitterness of sectarian prejudice must have been repellent to him, and was probably a cause of his lasting reluctance to affiliate with any sect."[5]

For most Christians today the Church is their chief avenue to strength in leading a Christian life and in offering God their worship. Bible reading and personal experience reinforce for them their basic orientation continuously being communicated through church life. This institutional element was lacking to a great degree in Lincoln. The Bible quite apart from the competing churches was his source of inspiration. Personal experience and reflection would give him ever deeper insights into the relevance of Scripture for personal decision and for understanding the meaning of history. The divisiveness of frontier denominationalism left a wound that never fully healed.

Any reservations Lincoln may have felt about the sectarian Christianity of New Salem would have been encouraged by association with another group of people in the neighborhood. These were called by their opponents "the infidels." They might have included Christians who wanted to reconcile the Bible with newer developments in science, rationalists who objected to the characteristic doctrines of the fighting sects, deists who advocated a religion of reason, humanists who argued that traditional religions endangered man's moral responsibility, and perhaps a few atheists of the village type. Any of these positions of dissent might also be labeled "atheist" by their opponents, who were not given to making precise differentiations in debate.

According to Herndon, Lincoln identified himself with this element in the community. There is undoubtedly some measure of truth here, but Herndon has got the picture badly out of focus. Later whispering campaigns against Lincoln as "an infidel," although untrue in their charge, must have been built on some positions taken by him at this time. Along with others in the community he apparently read Thomas Paine's *Age of Reason* and Volney's *Ruins,* discussing them cracker-barrel style around the fire at night. He became an enthusiastic member of a New Salem debating society in the winter of 1831–32. We are told that the club met twice a month with the chairman appointing the two debaters and assigning them their positions on the topic without regard to their own opinions on the matter. It is easy to see how positions on certain religious dogmas, taken simply for the purposes of debate by a brilliant youth in love with rhetoric and logic, might well be misunderstood later as expressing his own religious orientation. His handbill of 1846 describes a habit of arguing for some years in favor of "the doctrine of necessity."

Paine may well have spoken to Lincoln's doubts about the Bible. Many of these have ceased to be of concern for a modern Christian who accepts the methods of historical research in deal-

43

ing with biblical narratives. The way, however, to a historical interpretation of the Bible, still being pioneered among Christian scholars in that day, could not have been a live option in New Salem. Many of the arguments against, for example, Mosaic authorship of the first five books of the Bible would in his community have characterized a person as "an infidel." By the next generation most educated Christians would have accepted multiple authorship of these books without feeling the loss of anything really central to faith.

Volney's discussion of the rise and fall of empires may have given the young Lincoln the intellectual excitement of the march of history. Accompanying this awakened interest in history may well have come for a time a certain relativism about biblical authority. Within a few years he would meet a scholarly defense of the Bible that would show how "unhistorical" was Volney's thesis that Jesus Christ had never existed. There was an equally absurd thesis fathered by an English "infidel" named Taylor that the Jews had never been a historic people but were an order of freemasons. It is doubtful that Lincoln ever fundamentally accepted Paine's and Volney's skeptical positions. He probably found that on some special points he agreed with them against what passed as orthodoxy among the sects.

Those who side with Herndon in his confusing picture of Lincoln as now "an atheist," now "a deist," and now "a free-thinker" place great weight upon Lincoln's so-called "lost book on infidelity."[6] Always a very shaky thesis in the light of conflicting evidence, the tradition of the lost book was finally exploded by the discovery in 1941 of Lincoln's own statement denying in effect that he had ever held the "infidel" position.

44

The controversy about the "lost book" is worth, however, an examination. It drew forth from Lincoln's contemporaries fuller statements about his religious positions than can be found in any of his own documents for this period. Naturally they must be evaluated cautiously, for they were elicited by the bitter controversies following Holland's *Life*. The battle was renewed even more fiercely after Lamon's biography was published, largely from Herndon's collection of Lincoln material.[7]

Describing the impact of Paine and Volney upon the young storekeeper, Herndon wrote that "Lincoln read both these books, and assimilated them into his own being. He prepared an extended essay—called by many, a book—in which he made an argument against Christianity, striving to prove that the Bible was not inspired, and therefore not God's revelation, and that Jesus Christ was not the Son of God. The manuscript containing these audacious and comprehensive propositions he intended to have published or given a wide circulation in some other way. He carried it to the store, where it was read and freely discussed. His friend and employer, Samuel Hill, was among the listeners, and seriously questioning the propriety of a promising young man like Lincoln fathering such unpopular notions, he snatched the manuscript from his hands, and thrust it into the stove. The book went up in flames, and Mr. Lincoln's political future was secure. But his infidelity and his skeptical views were not diminished."[8]

No one ever offered direct evidence that he had himself read or heard read this supposed essay on "infidelity." There is another theory about the lost book reputedly burned by Hill. This version holds that youngsters in the village found a sizable letter written by Hill but somehow dropped by him. They returned it to Lincoln, the village postmaster, and as he was reading it aloud, possibly for purposes of identification, Hill, wanting to keep its contents a private matter, snatched the letter away and threw it into the flames. This version, however, has obvious difficulties.

Still another piece of testimony claims that Lincoln wrote an essay in defense of his own interpretation of Christianity. It would be easy in that contentious atmosphere to see how the later story of an infidel book might have grown up. In the light of Lincoln's own denial of infidelity in the handbill of 1846 this explanation has more to commend it than Herndon's dramatic tale or the "Hill letter" theory. It is further strengthened in coming directly from Mentor Graham, Lincoln's New Salem tutor and reputed helper in early speech writing.

". . . Abraham Lincoln was living at my house in New Salem, going to school, studying English grammar and surveying, in the year 1833. One morning he said to me, 'Graham, what do you think about the anger of the Lord?' I replied, 'I believe the Lord never was angry or mad and never would be; that His lovingkindness endures forever; that He never changes.' Said Lincoln, 'I have a little manuscript written, which I will show you'; and stated he thought of having it published. Offering it to me, he said he had never showed it to anyone, and still thought of having it published. The size of the manuscript was about one-half quire of foolscap, written in a very plain hand, on the subject of Christianity and a defense of universal salvation. The commencement of it was something respecting the God of the universe never being excited, mad, or angry. I had the manuscript in my possession some week or ten days. I have read many books on the subject of theology and I don't think in point of perspicuity and plainness of reasoning, I ever read one to surpass it. I remember well his argument. He took the passage, 'As in Adam all die, even so in Christ shall all be made alive,' and followed up with the proposition that whatever the breach or injury of Adam's transgressions to the human race was, which no doubt was very great, was made just and right by the atonement of Christ. . . ."[9]

This is hardly the statement of an "infidel" position. It reveals rather a mind dissatisfied with the sectarian theology of his community probing deeply into the Bible on its own. He wants to establish for himself a basic coherence between Christ's work as the Savior and God's ultimate plan for all mankind. Lincoln was actually in practice anticipating what would become the method of twentieth-century Christians. They would come to find God's word in the Bible although not everywhere identical with the words of the Bible.

Lincoln was questioning in this period the orthodox doctrine of scriptural authority by pressing on through "the logic of belief" to a deeper level. The unchanging affirmations for him in this process were man's need of salvation in terms of Adam's fall, God's loving purpose behind the infliction of punishment, and Christ's atoning work through his sacrificial death. Many of these themes would be repeated in later speeches or would provide the perspective for understanding his religious orientation.

These themes taken together in this New Salem period pointed him to the conviction, diametrically opposed to the popular Christian theology of his community, that God would through Christ ultimately save all men. Lincoln's doctrine of universal salvation through Christ would have seemed dangerous enough to the traditionally minded to warrant the label "infidel." To many this essay in defense of universalism in salvation would have been an "infidel book." These frontier preachers made the doctrine of endless punishment their chief whip to the leading of a good life on earth and to the acceptance in "faith" of the particular tenets of the sect.

Lincoln was probably led to his interpretation by two forces. First, the predestinarian cast of his youthful religious training convinced him, contrary to popular theology, that Christ's work had to become effectual to salvation for all men. If God had irresistibly decreed it, it would certainly come to pass. Secondly, Lincoln's rationalism required simple justice in the relations between God and man. He liked to repeat a jingle about the Indian Johnny Kongapod:

> "Here lies poor Johnny Kongapod.
> Have mercy on him, gracious God,
> As he would do if he was God
> And you were Johnny Kongapod."

The two forces of predestination and rationalism convinced him that salvation would be opened to all after proper reformatory punishment. It would not be restricted to a chosen few. The necessity in the first instance was that of logic, in the second that of ethics. Raised a predestinarian Baptist, Lincoln never became a Baptist, but he never ceased to be a predestinarian.

48

It is interesting to locate the section in Scripture which Lincoln used to support his interpretation of predestinated universal salvation. In the fifteenth chapter of I Corinthians, St. Paul describes a great cosmic restoration in the end-time. The first fruits of it are already present in the resurrection of Christ. Adam is responsible for the death that comes to all men, but Christ will deliver mankind from death into life everlasting in a cosmos purged of all opposition or resistance to the reign of God.

From the Graham statement and others made about Lincoln's belief in later years it would seem that Lincoln gave an absolute meaning to the phrase "in Christ shall all be made alive" quite apart from a number of qualifying themes in the Pauline passage.

"But now is Christ risen from the dead, and become the first-fruits of them that slept.

For since by man came death, by man came also the resurrection of the dead.

For as in Adam all die, even so in Christ shall all be made alive.

But every man in his own order: Christ the firstfruits; afterward they that are Christ's at his coming.

Then cometh the end, when he shall have delivered up the kingdom to God, even the Father; when he shall have put down all rule and all authority and power.

For he must reign, till he hath put all enemies under his feet. . . .

And when all things shall be subdued unto him, then shall the

Son also himself be subject unto him that put all things under him, that God may be all in all."[10]

The New Salem period, then, is hardly one of complete "infidelity," granting the conflicting meanings assigned to the word "infidel" at that time. This denial of the "infidel" position is in conflict with one held by many commentators. One group was determined to prove that Lincoln was once and always an "infidel." Another group was eager to stress a Prodigal Son period of grubbing in the husks of "infidelity" as a dramatic foil to a supposed later conversion to orthodox dogmatics. Both positions overstate the situation, although there are elements of truth badly out of focus in each. New Salem brought to Lincoln growing disillusionment with the fire and brimstone revivalists and their packaged theologies. Through doubts and questionings sharpened by discussions of Paine and Volney, Lincoln was struggling toward his own interpretation of God's purposes for man.

Lincoln occasionally stayed with the Rankin family in their home in Petersburg. Mrs. Rankin reported that he had had doubts at New Salem about his "former implicit faith in the Bible."

"Those days of trouble found me tossed amid a sea of questionings. They piled big upon me. . . . Through all I groped my way until I found a stronger and higher grasp of thought, one that reached beyond this life with a clearness and satisfaction I had never known before. The Scriptures unfolded before me with a deeper and more logical appeal, through these new experiences, than anything else I could find to turn to, or even before had found in them. I do not claim that all my doubts were removed then, or since that time have been swept away. They are not.

"Probably it is to be my lot to go on in a twilight, feeling and reasoning my way through life, as questioning, doubting Thomas did. But in my poor, maimed way, I bear with me as I go on a seeking spirit of desire for a faith that was with him of olden time, who, in his need, as I in mine, exclaimed, 'Help thou my unbelief.' "[11]

Then Lincoln added, "I doubt the possibility, or propriety, of settling the religion of Jesus Christ in the models of man-made creeds and dogmas. . . . I cannot without mental reservations assent to long and complicated creeds and catechisms."

Skepticism about the usefulness of dogma remained a settled conviction with him in adult life. It also partly explains why he never joined a church. These reservations about creeds, however, should not be understood as a denial of the biblical realities behind the dogmas. It was just because God and His purposes became so real to him that he felt no need for a dogmatic preservative or protective shell.

One of the ways in which Lincoln's faith was deepened was by making decisions about vocation and by committing himself to other people in responsible relationship. By this means he would come gradually to experience a sense of God's guidance in the events of personal life. The acceptance which he had won at New Salem whetted an appetite for politics, the fastest door at that time to success and recognition in a backwoods community. With this target in mind he set himself to the reading of law, borrowing legal books from many friends.

He decided to run for the state legislature and began a barnstorming campaign after his return from eight months' service in the Black Hawk War. His election as captain by his men pleased him greatly. He announced his platform in the *Sangamo Journal* on March 9, 1832. He favored internal improvements for the state, especially the deepening and straightening of the Sangamon River as less expensive than a railroad. He discussed the problems created by the loaning of money at exorbitant rates. Turning to education, he called it "the most important subject a people can be engaged in." It made it possible for men to study the history of their country. It gave them an appreciation of "the value of our free institutions . . . to say nothing of the advantages and satisfaction to be derived from all being able to read the Scriptures and other works, both of a religious and moral nature, for themselves."[12]

Then in a concluding paragraph he described his motivation in running for public office. "Every man is said to have his peculiar ambition. Whether it be true or not, I can say for one that I have no other so great as that of being truly esteemed of my fellow men, by rendering myself worthy of this esteem. How far I shall succeed in gratifying this ambition, is yet to be developed. I am young and unknown to many of you. I was born and have ever remained in the most humble walks of life. I have no wealthy or popular relations to recommend me. My case is thrown exclusively upon the independent voters of this county, and if elected they will have conferred a favor upon me, for which I shall be unremitting in my labors to compensate. But if the good people in their wisdom shall see fit to keep me in the background, I have been too familiar with disappointment to be very much chagrined."

Lincoln lost the election, running eighth of thirteen candidates, but his 277 of the 300 votes cast in the New Salem precinct were a sign of things to come. This defeat was his only one at the hands of the people. He turned again to the study of law.

His next attempt to be elected to the state legislature was successful and he served in all for four terms, becoming a member of the famous Long Nine in that body. He did the chores of a legislator faithfully and was instrumental in lining up support for the removal of the capital from Vandalia to Springfield.

When the legislature passed resolutions on the subject of slavery in terms of sacred property rights and with disapproval of abolitionist societies Lincoln and Dan Stone read a protest which was printed in the Journal of Proceedings. One of the tasks of this study will be to analyze Lincoln's religious opposition to slavery as it influenced his political positions on the issue. "They [Lincoln and Stone] believe that the institution of slavery is founded on both injustice and bad policy; but that the promulgation of abolition doctrines tends rather to increase than abate its evils. They believe that the Congress of the United States has no power, under the Constitution, to interfere with the institution of slavery in the different states."[13]

"Stand Still, and See the Salvation of the Lord"

Chapter 3

On April 15, 1837, on a borrowed horse and with his worldly possessions packed in his saddlebags, Lincoln rode into Springfield. Having passed his bar examinations, he was arriving to become the law partner of John T. Stuart, a polished Southerner who was already a powerful Whig leader. Lincoln's immediate future was secure and because of his influence in shifting the capital from Vandalia to Springfield he would be most acceptable to its progressive citizens.

Lincoln, however, was in a melancholy mood. Making his way to the store of Joshua Speed, a prosperous young merchant from an aristocratic Kentucky family, he asked how much the bedding and equipment for a single bedstead would cost. Dismayed at his resources, Lincoln said, "It is probably cheap enough; but I want to say that, cheap as it is, I have not the money to pay. But if you will credit me until Christmas, and my experiment here as a lawyer is a success, I will pay you then. If I fail in that I will probably never pay you at all."

Deeply moved by the melancholy face, Speed offered to share his quarters. "So small a debt seems to affect you so deeply, I think I can suggest a plan by which you will be able to attain your end without incurring any debt. I have a large room with a double bed upstairs, which you are welcome to share with me if you choose." Lincoln asked where the room was. Without a word he shouldered his saddlebags and went upstairs. Returning and smiling, he exclaimed, "Well, Speed, I'm moved."

With this incident began a deep friendship that lasted for life. The letters show a remarkable level of understanding and affectionate communication on such subjects as politics, women, and religion, still the hardy perennials in dormitory bull sessions. "When I knew him in early life," said Speed in a lecture after Lincoln's death, "he was a skeptic. He had tried hard to be a believer, but his reason could not grasp and solve the great problem of redemption as taught."

Lincoln's commitment to Speed passed beyond debate on things religious into a deepened experience of religious self-understanding. For four years these two roommates anxiously nursed each other over the humps in their courtship of the girls they left behind them and finally of the two they were to marry. Sandburg describes their friendship:

"Joshua Speed was a deep-chested man of large sockets, with broad measurement between the ears. A streak of lavender ran through him; he had spots soft as May violets. And he and Abraham Lincoln told each other their secrets about women.

56

Lincoln too had tough physical shanks and large sockets, also a streak of lavender, and spots soft as May violets.

" 'I do not feel my own sorrows more keenly than I do yours', Lincoln wrote to Speed in one letter. And again: 'You know my desire to befriend you is everlasting.' "[1]

Lincoln seems to have made some commitment close to an informal engagement with Mary Owens before settling in Springfield. He was miserable because he doubted whether he really loved her. Yet he felt bound to act according to honor. He described his melancholy to her. In one letter he revealed how a backwoods youth felt about the grand churches of Springfield with their settled pastors, their ordered worship, and their fashionable members. "I've never been to church yet, nor probably shall not soon. I stay away because I am conscious I should not know how to behave myself."[2]

The relationship with Mary Owens gradually petered out to the relief of both. Speed became the confidant of his friend in this matter as he would also share the ups and downs of a still more stormy courtship between Lincoln and Mary Todd.

There are two speeches of this period which are interesting from the point of view of future developments. The address of January 27, 1838, before the Young Men's Lyceum of Springfield suggests an understanding of the nation's history in comparison with religious institutions. Out of this small acorn would eventually grow a gnarled white oak resistant to wind and storm. The great Lincolnian theme of "this nation under God" would be anticipated formally, but as yet without dramatic content, in this essay, "The Perpetuation of Our Political Institutions."

57

"We find ourselves," he said, "under the government of a system of political institutions, conducing more essentially to the ends of civil and religious liberty, than any of which the history of former times tells us." He painted a picture of America as an impregnable fortress vulnerable only to violence from within. The lawlessness of the times was our greatest danger. He had doubtless chosen this subject because only three months before a howling mob had lynched the abolitionist editor Elijah Lovejoy at Alton, Illinois. His antidote for this was "reverence for the laws" which he wanted American mothers to breathe into "the lisping babe" and school and pulpit to inculcate. Then, using the metaphors of religion and its altars, he pleaded, "in short, let it become the *political religion* of the nation; and let the old and the young, the rich and the poor, the grave and the gay, of all sexes and tongues, and colors and conditions, sacrifice unceasingly upon its altars."

Americans had won their liberties by passionate feelings against injustice. They could no longer rely upon passion and the memory of the courageous actions of the Founding Fathers. Instead they must cultivate "cold, calculating reason." Here Lincoln manifested a strain of rationalism that was probably the by-product of a man of meager background struggling to become self-educated. It is interesting to find Lincoln dismissing those memories of a shared past that give continuity to a nation's history in favor of "calculating reason." In his more mature years he would evoke as no other speaker has ever done the "mystic chords of memory, stretching from every battlefield and patriot grave, to every living heart and hearthstone, all over this broad land."

Later on Lincoln would understand the nation's history in a continuity of purpose with the acts of God as interpreted by the biblical prophets. Here he offers something else. "Passion has helped us; but can do so no more. It will in future be our enemy. Reason, cold, calculating, unimpassioned reason, must furnish all the materials for our future support and defense. Let those (materials) be molded into *general intelligence*, (*sound*) *morality* and, in particular, *a reverence for the constitution and laws. . . .*" Then, reverting to the earlier parallelism, he closes: "Upon these let the proud fabric of freedom rest, as the rock of its basis; and as truly as has been said of the only greater institution, *'the gates of hell shall not prevail against it.'* "[3]

On Washington's Birthday in 1842, Lincoln delivered an address in the Second Presbyterian Church to the Washington Temperance Society. The speech shows such an intimate acquaintance with biblical language and incidents that, had its authorship been unknown, scholars would probably have assigned it to one professionally trained in the field of biblical study. While its perspective was a deep Christian compassion for one's fellow man, it rubbed many church members the wrong way. They just did not like having their virtue over against the drunkard explained away as "absence of appetite" rather than commended as "mental or moral superiority." Lincoln's political popularity suffered in a subsequent election partly, as he believed, because of this speech.

Lincoln began by accepting the principle of our present-day Alcoholics Anonymous, namely, that the reformed drunkard is himself the most persuasive helper for the alcoholic. Preachers and hired agents, Lincoln affirmed, had as a class a want of approachability fatal to their success. He criticized a temperance strategy that condemned the liquor manufacturer and merchant as the chief devils and showed no concern for dealing with present drunkards. Blazing condemnation thundered from pulpit and platform failed utterly to convince the wayward. It only alienated them because it was predicated on "a reversal of human nature, which is God's decree, and never can be reversed." He pointed out that the true approach to winning a man was first to "convince him that you are his sincere friend. Therein is a drop of honey that catches his heart, which, say what he will, is the great high road to his reason, and which, when once gained, you will find but little trouble in convincing his judgment of the justice of your cause, if indeed that cause really be a just one."

Not only was the widespread temperance program of denunciation impolitic. Lincoln argued that it was also unjust. This approach would have alienated those for whom moral questions were simple absolutes divorced from their total setting in life. Lincoln's point was that temperance reform was so new and the acceptance by mankind of drinking so universal in history and still the majority sentiment that the method of denunciation affronted men's opinions. In his development of this point he reveals an interesting attitude toward rational proof for God's existence. "The universal *sense* of mankind, on any subject, is an argument, or at least an *influence,* not easily overcome. The success of the argument in favor of the existence of an overruling Providence, mainly depends upon that sense; and men ought not, in justice, to be denounced for yielding to it in any case, or for giving it up slowly, *especially,* where they are backed by interest, fixed habits, or burning appetites."

Lincoln then turned to the highest ground in seeking to persuade his hearers that those who had never been afflicted with alcoholism should not refuse to join a society of reformed drunkards. His point was that the Washingtonian's compassion for the alcoholic was the same expression of concerned love that led a sovereign Creator to incarnate Himself in the form of man.

" 'But,' say some, 'we are no drunkards; and we shall not acknowledge ourselves such by joining a reformed drunkards' society, whatever our influence might be.' Surely no Christian will adhere to this objection. If they believe, as they profess, that Omnipotence condescended to take on himself the form of sinful man, and as such, to die an ignominious death for their sakes, surely they will not refuse submission to the infinitely lesser condescension, for the temporal, and perhaps eternal salvation, of a large, erring, and unfortunate class of their own fellow creatures. Nor is the condescension very great."

Some writers, intent on proving Lincoln a "freethinker," claim that Lincoln's use of "they" in this paragraph expresses his rejection of Christianity. It is a wrong conclusion for the simple reason that the word "they" is stylistic in use. A few paragraphs before Lincoln used "they" of the Washingtonians, the very group of which he was a member and to which he was speaking. Lincoln's whole setting of his essay is that the Washingtonian approach is the deeply Christian one of the incarnational principle. From this deeper Christian position he argues against the Christian pharisee of his day.

The essay concludes, however, on another note. There is a deification of "Reason," now somewhat more warmly commended than in the Lyceum address, in which the reason was of the "cold, calculating" type. There is, however, a hollow ring to his rhetorical peroration. Developments in his personal life would very soon convince him of the need for more than reason to solve personal dilemmas. From here the new openness would spread gradually to his interpretation of man's future. In this temperance address the analysis is biblically oriented, the program of action deeply Christian in context, but the motivation still remains rationalistic. "Happy day, when, all appetites controlled, all passions subdued, all matters subjected, *mind,* all-conquering *mind,* shall live and move the monarch of the world. Glorious consummation! Hail, fall of Fury! Reign of Reason, all hail!"[4]

Lincoln's bombastic apostrophe to "Reason" may have been a whistling in the dark, a self-prescription which he hoped would stabilize the deep unrest and melancholy within him. Having wriggled out of a commitment to Mary Owens, he soon found himself pledged to Mary Todd, a vivacious and cultured Kentuckian who had come to live with her sister, Mrs. Ninian W. Edwards, in Springfield. Coming from a genteel social background in Lexington, educated in the exclusive school of Madame Mentelle, Mary Todd enjoyed a wide popularity among the young bachelors who were admitted into the Edwards' social circle.

Abraham and Mary, perhaps because of the attraction of opposites, hit it off at once. They became engaged. Then something separated them on January 1, 1841. Herndon tells a vivid tale of the bride deserted at the altar, but the evidence points rather to Lincoln's breaking the engagement himself. He had become miserable in a siege of depression and doubted whether he could be happy with Mary or whether he could make her happy. Released apparently by Mary from his promise, instead of getting a hold on himself he burrowed ever more deeply in his gloom.

A glimpse into the blackness of his despair is afforded by letters to his friend John T. Stuart, then in Washington, imploring him to secure the postmastership at Springfield for his doctor. "I have, within the last few days, been making a most discreditable exhibition of myself in the way of hypochondriasm and thereby got an impression that Dr. Henry is necessary to my existence. Unless he gets that place he leaves Springfield. You therefore see how much I am interested in the matter."[5]

A second letter three days later further spelled out his agony. "I am now the most miserable man living. If what I feel were equally distributed to the whole human family, there would not be one cheerful face on the earth. Whether I shall ever be better, I cannot tell; I awfully forbode I shall not. To remain as I am is impossible; I must die or be better, it appears to me."[6]

The situation of the wretched suitor became even more lonely when Speed early in 1841 sold out his business and returned to Kentucky. He did, however, persuade Lincoln to visit him on the family plantation near Louisville from early August to mid-September. On his return Lincoln wrote to Joshua's half sister, referring to the Oxford Bible Speed's mother had given him: "I intend to read it regularly when I return home." Then he added, perhaps somewhat wistfully, "I doubt not that it is really, as she says, the best cure for the 'Blues' could one but take it according to the truth."[7]

Then occurred a change that brought a reversal of roles and made Lincoln counselor to Speed, now engaged to Fanny Henning. Drawn out of preoccupation with his own problems, in helping Speed, he began to help himself. Lincoln's reassuring letters comforted his friend's "nervous debility" and his questioning whether he was really in love with his fiancée.

When an illness of Fanny's frightened Speed into gloomy forebodings about her death Lincoln revealed his belief in God's immediate concern with and control over personal life. Lincoln argued that his friend's anguish over the possibility of his fiancée's death was clear evidence of his love for her. "I almost feel a presentiment that the Almighty has sent your present affliction expressly for that object. . . . Should she, as you fear, be destined to an early grave, it is indeed a great consolation to know that she is so well prepared to meet it. Her religion, which you once disliked so much, I will venture you now prize most highly."[8]

When Lincoln learned that the happiness of his newly married friend exceeded his expectation, he was overjoyed. It brought him more pleasure than had been his lot since "that fatal first Jany. '41" when he had asked to be released from his engagement to Mary Todd. "Since then, it seems to me, I should have been entirely happy, but for the never-absent idea, that there is *one* still unhappy whom I have contributed to make so. That still kills my soul. I cannot but reproach myself, for even wishing to be happy while she is otherwise. She accompanied a large party on the Rail Road cars, to Jacksonville last Monday; and on her return, spoke, so that I heard of it, of having enjoyed the trip exceedingly. God be praised for that."[9]

In another letter some months later Lincoln acknowledged the correctness of his friend's advice about his own unhappy situation with respect to Mary Todd: ". . . but before I resolve to do the one thing or the other, I must regain my confidence in my own ability to keep my resolves when they are made. In that ability, you know, I once prided myself . . ." Then he introduced the religious dimension. By less preoccupation with his own problem and by more reliance on God's guidance of his circumstances he expected to reach a solution. This religious awakening he clothed in predestinarian garb.

"The truth is, I am not sure there was any merit, with me, in the part I took in your difficulty; I was drawn to it as by fate; if I would, I could not have done less than I did." Then he gave a firm religious orientation to his fatalism. "I always was superstitious; and as part of my superstition, I believe God made me one of the instruments of bringing your Fanny and you together, which union, I have no doubt He had foreordained." Turning from the past and the belief that God foreordained his friend's marriage, he expressed for the immediate future a quiet acceptance of the deliverance that God's predestinating activity would bring him. "Whatever he designs, he will do for *me* yet. 'Stand *still*, and see the salvation of the Lord' is my text just now."[10]

Ruth Painter Randall in her charming *Courtship of Mr. Lincoln* finds evidence here of a sense of religious dependence often to reappear in the future. "It often happens that people who have come through a long, baffling siege of the spirit, grappling with problems that seem to have no solution, unable to decide which course of action to take, cease struggling to turn to their religious faith and rest their weary souls in waiting for a revelation of divine guidance. Such was Lincoln's state now. He was a man of deep religious feeling. All the rest of his life one finds incidents in which he placed his reliance on the will of God."[11]

The resolution of his love for Mary Todd was not to come, however, without a jolting experience that had all the features of a television re-creation of nineteenth-century romance. He nearly had to fight a duel, a situation which later on in life mortified him so deeply that he would never discuss the incident. The long and short of a very involved tale is that Lincoln wrote an anonymous letter to a local newspaper from a "Rebecca of the Lost Townships." In it he attacked a political rival, James Shields, very unfairly and with withering sarcasm. Others also wrote abusive letters under the same pseudonym, one coming from Mary Todd and a friend of hers.

Shields, a truculent Irishman, charged the whole authorship to Lincoln, who chivalrously would not reveal Mary's part in it. Although contrary to the law of Illinois, Lincoln felt he had to accept Shields's challenge to duel. The altercation was finally adjusted at the field proposed for combat. The episode, with its anonymous attacks on opponents comparable to *The Chronicles of Reuben*, reveals some of that raw frontier background. In later life Lincoln would learn the lesson of responsible opposition to his political adversaries without underhanded attacks and personal vilification. The immediate result of the code duello appears to have brought Abraham and Mary together again.

Once more he sought Speed's help in reassuring his own doubts. He wrote his friend on October 5, 1842, "to say something on that subject which you know to be of such infinite solicitude to me. The immense suffering you endured from the first days of September till the middle of February you never tried to conceal from me, and I well understood. You have now been the husband of a lovely woman nearly eight months. That you are happier now than you were the day you married her I well know; for without, you would not be living. But I have your word for it too; and the returning elasticity of spirits which is manifested in your letters. But I want to ask a closer question— 'Are you now, in *feeling* as well as *judgment*, glad you are married as you are?' From anybody but me, this would be an impudent question not to be tolerated; but I know you will pardon it in me. Please answer it quickly as I feel impatient to know."[12]

Within a month, on November 4, 1842, Abraham and Mary were married in the Edwards' parlor with an Episcopal clergyman, the Rev. Charles Dresser, performing the ceremony.

There are at least two levels on which the marriage had significance for Lincoln's religious development. On the first level it brought Lincoln as a family man closer to conventional church relationships. Mary attended the Episcopal Church in Springfield and he accompanied her at times. After the death of their son Edward, Mary became a member of the Presbyterian Church. Her Episcopal rector had been out of town and the funeral service was performed for the sorrowing parents by the Rev. James Smith of the First Presbyterian Church. Lincoln became a regular attendant from that time on. Later, from the White House, Mrs. Lincoln wrote back to Springfield asking that "our particular pew" might be reserved for them until their return. Mary's religion clutched at tangible securities like the family pew.

The second level of religious influence exerted by the marriage was upon Lincoln's character. While the marriage was stable and blessed with mutual affection and comfort, there was also a darker side to it. Mary had a towering rage, was unduly concerned over little things, and seemed unable to achieve a satisfactory relationship to the children, now indulging them too much and now dealing far too harshly with them. There were already in Mary some of the tragic symptoms that after her cruel bereavements of three children and husband would require institutional care. Lincoln adored his children to the point of indulging them. At times he had to leave the house when Mary's anger and hysteria became too sharp. He learned forbearance and forgiveness, not as doctrines but in practice. Through it all Lincoln achieved a serenity of faith and a deepened understanding far beyond the level of his wife's. She had had perhaps greater initial commitment to the Christian faith than he had. Part of the tragedy of Mary Todd is that she did not have her husband's capacities for growth. Limited by the structure of an abnormal personality, her own faith seems brittle beside the flowering of his.

"Now Convinced of the Truth of the Christian Religion"

Chapter 4

Lincoln's race for Congress in 1846 was having its ups and downs. With only a few days left before the election, reports were reaching Lincoln that his political opponent on the Democratic ticket was whispering the charge of "infidelity" against him in the northern counties. Lincoln was accused of being a scoffer at religion.

Lincoln knew what this could mean for him. It had cost him a nomination once before in 1843. He had conducted a post-mortem of that Whig convention in a letter to Martin Morris: ". . . it was everywhere contended that no Christian ought to go for me, because I belonged to no church, was suspected of being a deist, and had talked about fighting a duel. With all these things Baker, of course, had nothing to do. Nor do I complain of them. As to his own church going for him, I think that was right enough, and as to the influences I have spoken of in the other, though they were very strong, it would be grossly untrue and unjust to charge that they acted upon them in a body or even very nearly so. I only mean that those influences levied a tax of considerable per cent upon my strength throughout the religious community."[1] He might have added that his temperance address had offended many.

The trouble now, however, was considerably more acute, for the charge was being made by no less a person than the popular, rugged Peter Cartwright, twenty-four years his elder and widely known all over Illinois. This excitable Methodist circuit rider was as strong in body as he was resourceful in spirit. Many times he had interrupted his revivalist message to collar some heckler or drunkard and toss him out of the meeting, returning to the stump with the words, "As I was saying . . ." Even the saints were not safe from chastisement. He rebuked a deacon who had offered a formal prayer: "Brother, three prayers like that would freeze hell over." Refuting a sermon on the indefectibility of grace, he gathered his hearers under a tree. Saying, "I promised I'd answer those who believe once in grace always in grace," he leaped up and hung for a minute to an overhanging limb. Then he let go, fell to the ground, and walked away, his sermon finished.

Sandburg paints a dramatic picture of an encounter that was supposed to have taken place between the two political rivals in the campaign.

"In spite of warnings he went anyhow to a religious meeting where Cartwright was to preach. In due time Cartwright said,

'All who desire to lead a new life, to give their hearts to God, and go to heaven, will stand,' and a sprinkling of men, women, and children stood up. Then the preacher exhorted, 'All who do not wish to go to hell will stand.' All stood up—except Lincoln. Then said Cartwright in his gravest voice, 'I observe that many responded to the first invitation to give their hearts to God and go to heaven. And I further observe that all of you save one indicated that you did not desire to go to hell. The sole exception is Mr. Lincoln, who did not respond to either invitation. May I inquire of you, Mr. Lincoln, where you are going?'

"And Lincoln slowly rose and slowly spoke, 'I came here as a respectful listener. I did not know that I was to be singled out by Brother Cartwright. I believe in treating religious matters with due solemnity. I admit that the questions propounded by Brother Cartwright are of great importance. I did not feel called upon to answer as the rest did. Brother Cartwright asks me directly where I am going. I desire to reply with equal directness: I am going to Congress.' The meeting broke up."[2]

The immediate threat from his antagonist's charge of "infidelity" lay in the fact that the time before the election was short. The charge, moreover, was not a public one. It was difficult to answer. Probably the damage was not yet widespread, but it might be dangerous not to do anything about it. Lincoln disliked intensely having to take public notice of it. He did not want to discuss his religion on the stump, but he also did not want to lose his chance to go to Washington.

His first strategy was to write friends in the northern counties a contradiction of Cartwright's charge, requesting that "they should publish it or not, as in their discretion they might think proper, having in view the extent of the circulation of the charge, as also the extent of credence it might be receiving." His friends decided not to publish Lincoln's statement. Then Lincoln learned that the whispering campaign had spread into other counties. With the election coming up on August 3, he had a handbill printed on July 31.

Within a few days the suspense was over. While Cartwright was a most effective evangelist he turned out to be a poor candidate for Congress. Lincoln received a sizable victory of 6340 votes over Cartwright's 4829. A reading of the returns, however, for Marshall and Woodford counties, which Cartwright had carried by decisive margins, led Lincoln to set the record straight for the future. He wrote to Allen Ford, the editor of the *Illinois Gazette*, about a week after the election asking that both letter and handbill be published in his paper. He strengthened the contents of his public statement by adding, "I here aver, that he, Cartwright, never heard me utter a word in any way indicating my opinions on religious matters, in his life."[8]

One of the most exciting discoveries in Lincoln scholarship was the finding of this letter and handbill by Harry E. Pratt in 1941. It demolished earlier interpretations which had tried to make Lincoln out an atheist or a deist. It is the only public document, moreover, in which Lincoln ever gave personal testimony about his religious views. The handbill is an authoritative refutation by Lincoln of the charge of "infidelity." It both casts light backward on the confusion of the New Salem period and provides motifs for understanding developments in the future. Its importance, however, must be limited by the qualification that here Lincoln speaks for 1846, not 1865. The fact that Lincoln was denying false charges made against him gives the document a necessarily negative character. He revealed just enough of his own religious orientation to make the required refutation. Beyond this minimum he offered very little. Hence it would not be correct to draw as a necessary conclusion, as a number of writers have, that Lincoln believed nothing beyond these statements. He was a politician refuting a local libel in this handbill, not a confessor delivering a testament of faith to all mankind.

"July 31, 1846

"TO THE VOTERS OF THE SEVENTH CONGRESSIONAL DISTRICT
"Fellow Citizens:

A charge having got into circulation in some of the neighborhoods of this District, in substance that I am an open scoffer at Christianity, I have by the advice of some friends concluded to notice the subject in this form. That I am not a member of any Christian Church, is true; but I have never denied the truth of the Scriptures; and I have never spoken with intentional disrespect of religion in general, or of any denomination of Christians in particular. It is true that in early life I was inclined to believe in what I understand is called the 'Doctrine of Necessity'—that is, that the human mind is impelled to action, or held in rest by some power, over which the mind itself has no control; and I have sometimes (with one, two or three, but never publicly) tried to maintain this opinion in argument. The habit of arguing thus however, I have, entirely left off for more than five years. And I add here, I have always understood this same opinion to be held by several of the Christian denominations. The foregoing, is the whole truth, briefly stated, in relation to myself, upon this subject.

73

"I do not think I could myself, be brought to support a man for office, whom I knew to be an open enemy of, and scoffer at, religion. Leaving the higher matter of eternal consequences, between him and his Maker, I still do not think any man has the right thus to insult the feelings, and injure the morals, of the community in which he may live. If, then, I was guilty of such conduct, I should blame no man who should condemn me for it; but I do blame those, whoever they may be, who falsely put such a charge in circulation against me."[4]

Here we find Lincoln publicly stating that he was not a church member. He never became one. Mrs. Rankin, who has already been quoted, recalled that Lincoln had stayed in her house at Petersburg about June of 1846. Lincoln spoke again of his reservations about "the possibility and propriety of settling the religion of Jesus Christ in the models of man-made creeds and dogmas." He then said something that he was accustomed to repeat throughout the rest of his life. The substance of it was that he would join a church that made the Savior's summary of the law of love to God and to neighbor its condition of membership. This apparently became a settled conviction with him as seen from his statement to Congressman Deming, who reported it in his address before the General Assembly of Connecticut in 1865:

"I am here reminded of an impressive remark he made to me upon another occasion, and which I shall never forget. He said, he had never united himself to any church, because he found difficulty in giving his assent, without mental reservations, to the long complicated statements of Christian doctrine which characterize their Articles of Belief and Confessions of Faith.

74

'When any church,' he continued, 'will inscribe over its altar as its sole qualification for membership the Savior's condensed statement of the substance of both the law and Gospel, Thou shalt love the Lord thy God with all thy heart, and with all thy soul, and with all thy mind, and thy neighbor as thyself,— that Church will I join with all my heart and soul.' "[5]

In his document of 1846, Lincoln immediately qualified his denial of church membership with the clause "but I have never denied the truth of the Scriptures." As we have seen before, the Bible rather than the Church remained his highroad to the knowledge of God. An interesting and important deepening of his trust in the Bible would shortly take place.

He did not like creedal tests for membership. This must not be interpreted to mean that he believed in a religion without content in the terms of a widespread contemporary approval of "creedless" religion, i.e., religiousness in general. Lincoln's beliefs were deeply biblical in their rootage. It was just because he took so seriously "the truth of the Scriptures" that he objected to man-made abstracts. His impatience with frontier squabbles over the minutiae of denominational differences doubtless was a strong conditioning element behind this conviction. Such contentious debates, he knew, obscured the essential emphasis of "the Savior" upon a faith that bore fruits.

Lincoln may not have sufficiently appreciated the necessity for a historical faith like Christianity to embody its central experience in creeds to help make it transmissible from one generation to another. He did, however, clearly see the danger of a creedal denominationalism that lacked love.

He further added in the handbill of 1846 that he had never

spoken "with intentional disrespect of religion in general, or of any denomination of Christians in particular." There is evidence that from the time of his presidency he came to have a more affectionate regard for the churches. His many responses to visiting delegations showed this. Fairly typical was his statement to the Methodists under Bishop Ames: "God bless the Methodist Church—bless all the churches—and blessed be God, Who, in this our great trial, giveth us the churches."[6]

Apparently aware of some of the tinder used by his opponents to kindle their charge of "infidelity," Lincoln explained his changing perspectives on what he understood was called the "Doctrine of Necessity." The issue here is not immediately clear. He defined his understanding of the phrase, about which he once debated in small groups, as the belief "that the human mind is impelled to action, or held in rest by some power, over which the mind itself has no control."

This definition by itself describes fatalism. Herndon said he was a fatalist. Henry C. Whitney, who rode with him on the circuit, wrote, "Mr. Lincoln was a fatalist: he believed, and often said, that 'There's a divinity that shapes our ends, Roughhew them how we will.' "[7] Mrs. Lincoln interpreted her husband's lack of concern about threats of assassination as a conviction that he would die when it was foreordained. In a letter to Speed already quoted, Lincoln describes himself as a fatalist. To Congressman Arnold he said much later: "I have been all my life a fatalist," quoting Shakespeare's lines once again.

There are, however, many types of fatalism. They shade on the right from the view that God's will determines every event in man's life all the way over to the left with the view that in a universe of ironbound cause and effect all human actions are determined. The poles are theological predestination and philosophical determinism. Herndon catches the original religious rootage of this idea for Lincoln in the predestinarian debates among the Baptists in the churches of his childhood and youth. "His early Baptist training made him a fatalist to the day of his death. . . ."[8]

What probably happened is that Lincoln in the New Salem period revolted against the harsh predestinarian conclusions about the fate of unbelievers. He may have sought to restate the "Doctrine of Necessity" in more philosophical terms. Perhaps, as Roy Basler suggests, he was influenced by a climate of opinion stemming from William Godwin's *Political Justice*. Godwin, once a Calvinist, crossed his "Doctrine of Necessity" with ideas of human perfectibility from the French Enlightenment.

This interpretation would be consistent with Lincoln's appeal to "cold, calculating reason" and with his "deification" of "Reason" in the temperance address. Yet these appeals taken at face value would argue a view of the freedom of man's mind to choose and act by itself. This would, of course, conflict with Lincoln's statement in the handbill that he "was inclined to believe" in the "Doctrine of Necessity." The inconsistency here is a real one and Lincoln never clearly resolved the issue philosophically. The weight, however, was on the side of determination.

This can be proved by the very way he came to express his difference with the traditional theology of eternal damnation. Mentor Graham's statement shows that Lincoln's view of a universal restoration was predicated upon God's determining action: "In Christ shall all be made alive." This structural element of determination remained constant in Lincoln's thought. He would later describe the way God worked upon men's minds and upon their actions in terms nearly identical with those of the handbill. "The will of God prevails. . . . By His mere quiet power, on the minds of the now contestants, He could have either *saved* or *destroyed* the Union without a human contest."[9]

The direction of Lincoln's religious fatalism beyond the period of the handbill would be toward a deeper understanding of the biblical stress upon God's will and upon his own responsibility as "God's instrument." Although the Bible would be his primary inspiration for this insight he may have been helped somewhat in its articulation by the Calvinistic doctrine of predestination as expounded by two distinguished Old-School Presbyterian pastors under whom he would sit in Springfield and in Washington.

This is not to state that Lincoln accepted the system of Calvinism. It is merely to point out that Presbyterian preaching on this theme may have helped him to give greater logical precision to a fundamental insight acquired in youth from his Baptist environment, modified in a philosophical direction in New Salem and in the early years at Springfield, and again reestablished in his later life as a primary biblical belief of his own.

In the handbill of 1846, as though to lessen any possible exploitation by his political opponents of his "Doctrine of Necessity" as a sign of Infidelity, Lincoln adds: "I have always understood this same opinion to be held by several of the

78

Christian denominations." He goes on to point out that he himself could not support for public office a man he "knew to be an open enemy of, and scoffer at, religion."

This statement alone demolishes the numerous attempts to paint Lincoln as a "freethinker," unless of course the theory is held that everything Lincoln said about God and his faith was politically motivated deception. Such a bizarre theory contradicts the one fundamental trait that all find in Lincoln—a bedrock of integrity. Even if the theory be entertained for the sake of argument, it is completely self-defeating because a man of Lincoln's intelligence could have done a much better job of deceiving religious people by greater conformity to conventional religion than he ever showed.

From the point of view of advancing Lincoln's political career, his term in the House of Representatives was a definite failure. The chief reason for this lay in the resolutions he introduced into the House demanding to know the "spot" where the Mexican War had started. He held Democratic President Polk responsible for starting the war unconstitutionally. Lincoln's attitude was decidedly unpopular at home where expansionist sentiment was rampant. On his return to Illinois he also discovered that he had lost any power of patronage from his own Whig party. He therefore turned away from politics and concentrated on his practice of the law.

"The decision," writes Benjamin Thomas, "made the years of his political retirement, from 1849 to 1854, among the most fruitful of his life. For as he put aside all thought of political advancement and devoted himself to personal improvement, he grew tremendously in mind and character."[10]

The Lincoln family, with its breadwinner increasingly successful as a lawyer of wide reputation, was suddenly brought up short against the cruel accidents of life. Their second son Edward Baker died on February 1, 1850, just under the age of four, after an illness of fifty-two days. The grief-stricken parents, unable to locate the Episcopal clergyman who had married them and whose church they occasionally attended, turned to the Rev. James Smith of the First Presbyterian Church to conduct the funeral. A rugged Scotsman with a fine mind and an interesting fund of anecdotes, he was a helpful pastor to the bereaved parents. The Lincolns soon took a pew with an annual rental of fifty dollars and became regular attendants. Mrs. Lincoln became a member.

The loss of Eddie turned Lincoln's thoughts to the great question of life after death. He had known the dreadful emptiness that came to a sobbing nine-year-old boy when his mother had died in that Indiana cabin. Again he felt the chill hand of death when his sister died shortly after her marriage. There is evidence that he felt keenly the death of Ann Rutledge at New Salem. These experiences, added to the tendency toward melancholy in his nature, explain his fondness for poetry that expressed the transience of life, its subjection to sudden changes in fortune, and its vulnerability before death. He said many times that his favorite poem was William Knox's *Oh, Why Should the Spirit of Mortal Be Proud?* although he did not know the author. He quoted Grey's *Elegy*, liked Holmes's *Last Leaf*, and earlier had tried to express his own feelings of sad fatalism in verse:

> "I range the fields with pensive tread,
>   And pace the hollow rooms;
>   And feel (companions of the dead)
> I'm living in the tombs."[11]

A few days after the funeral there appeared in the *Illinois Journal* these unsigned lines entitled *Little Eddie*.

> The angel death was hovering nigh,
> And the lovely boy was called to die.
> Bright is the home to him now given,
> For "of such is the kingdom of heaven."

They were probably written by Abraham or Mary, especially since they had the phrase "Of such is the Kingdom of Heaven" engraved on Edward Baker's white marble stone.

The clearest expression we have of Lincoln's view of personal immortality comes less than a year after Eddie's death in a letter to his stepbrother John Johnston when he heard of the serious illness of his father. The letter suggests strained relations between father and son, but closes on a deeply biblical note. "I sincerely hope Father may yet recover his health; but at all events tell him to remember to call upon, and confide in, our great, and good, and merciful Maker; who will not turn away from him in any extremity. He notes the fall of a sparrow, and numbers the hairs of our heads; and He will not forget the dying man, who puts his trust in Him. Say to him that if we could meet now, it is doubtful whether it would not be more painful than pleasant; but that if it is to be his lot to go now, he will soon have a joyous [meeting] with many loved ones gone before; and where [the rest] of us, through the help of God, hope ere-long [to join] them."[12]

A strong friendship grew up between Lincoln and his pastor Dr. Smith that lasted until Lincoln's death. Describing Smith to Seward as "an intimate personal friend of mine," he appointed him American consul at Dundee when the distinguished preacher retired to his native Scotland. After Lincoln's death the family sent Dr. Smith one of the President's gold-headed canes as a token of their esteem and affection.

More significant, however, for Lincoln's religious development was the intellectual challenge of his friend's mind. Shortly after Eddie's death the Lincolns went to Kentucky to stay with the Todd relatives. Here Lincoln found and partly read a learned work entitled *The Christian's Defense* by the Rev. James Smith, published in Cincinnati in 1843.

The book was the product of three weeks of formal debates at Columbus, Mississippi, between the author and a popular "freethinker" named Olmstead. The author was, of course, the man who had comforted them in bereavement. This personal tie and the drama of the religious debate undoubtedly drew Lincoln's interest. Upon his return to Springfield Lincoln secured a copy of the book and studied it carefully.

Dr. Smith described the result to Herndon, who had written to him in Scotland. "It was my honor to place before Mr. Lincoln arguments designed to prove the divine authority and inspiration of the Scriptures, accompanied by the arguments of infidel objectors in their own language. To the arguments on both sides Mr. Lincoln gave a most patient, impartial, and searching investigation. To use his own language, he examined the arguments as a lawyer who is anxious to investigate truth investigates testimony. The result was the announcement made by himself that the argument in favor of the divine authority and inspiration of the Scriptures was unanswerable."[13]

This 600-page tome is worthy of careful study, for it is one of the very few technical books on theology read by Lincoln. Despite the discovery of new archaeological evidence and the acceptance of quite different historical perspectives than those available then, the book is still an interesting study. Most of the defenses of Christianity in that day were addressed to the already converted. From his frontier background Lincoln knew the abuse heaped upon the "infidel" in standard dogmatics. Rather than be given an answer, he would be consigned to Satan.

But here was a welcome change. The author had himself been a skeptic. He quoted extensively from Paine, Volney, Robert Taylor, and other objectors to the authority of the Bible. Lincoln was himself beginning to quote more from his opponents as a preliminary to fairer and more effective rebuttal. Smith then endeavored to give a logical and even legal reply according to rules of testimony. This two-way conversation apparently interested Lincoln a great deal. In an appendix Dr. Smith drew from a standard legal work, Starkie's *Practical Treatise on the Law of Evidence,* to refute Hume's arguments about testimony.

Here Lincoln found convincing explanations of some of the points made by Paine and Volney that may have troubled him through the years. While the author's answers contain much that could not be accepted today they were advanced then in good faith. There was an attempt to show that modern geological discoveries and classical historians both constituted external testimony to the truth of Scripture. Since the language of the Bible was at times metaphorical it was unreasonable, urged Dr. Smith, to demand that it speak like Newtonian science.

It was argued that God accommodated Himself in revelation to the cultural level of his people, suggesting thereby a view of development that the author never articulated himself. He did, however, have a feeling for the sweep of human history from its earliest beginnings. The history of the Jews and of the early Christian community were the keys to its understanding. Illustrations of the significance of holidays like Independence Day for the American people were creatively used to show how Sunday was the celebration of the Christian act of redemption. There is no wall between an embalmed "sacred" history and current "secular" history. History is all of one piece, with the Bible its key.

There are some interesting parallels between positions advanced by Dr. Smith and those later stated by Lincoln. Whether or not there is direct influence is incapable of proof at this date. The author's argument that the universal practice of sacrifice is a testimony to the Atonement can serve both as a sample of his writing and as an illustration of a possible area of influence. The Honorable Orlando Kellogg came to the

White House in the interests of a wounded soldier who had previously deserted. Lincoln, granting a pardon, asked a question: "Kellogg . . . isn't there something in Scripture about the 'shedding of blood' being 'the remission of sins'?"

"Is there," argued Dr. Smith, "any rational mode of explaining the universality of this practice save that it originated in a divine appointment . . . and that it continued to be regarded as a divine institution wherever the true God was known, until its whole design was consummated in the voluntary offering up of Christ himself at Calvary! Admit this view of the case, and the whole history of animal sacrifice is plain and satisfactory. The providence of God, watching over the perpetuity of his own institutions, secures the universal observance of this practice; and in the practice itself we have the great leading principle of his government, as exercised towards a fallen and guilty race, 'that without the shedding of blood there is no remission.' "[14]

More significant, however, than parallels in content is the possibility of a direct influence in method. Smith's procedure was to establish everything that he could in Scripture by the use of reason before appealing to faith. Lincoln apparently felt in his New Salem years and for some time after that reason and faith were opposed to each other. Increasingly he came to regard them as complementary. His own clearest statement about the interrelations of reason and faith was made to Speed in the summer of 1864. Finding Lincoln reading the Bible in his room at the Soldiers' Home, Speed said, "If you have recovered from your skepticism, I am sorry to say that I have not." Then, reported Speed, "Looking me earnestly in the face, and placing his hand on my shoulder, he said, 'You are wrong, Speed; take all of this Book upon reason that you can, and the balance on faith, and you will live and die a happier and better man.' "[15]

Thomas Lewis, a Springfield lawyer and deacon of the church Lincoln attended, and John T. Stuart, his early law partner, both spoke of the impact of Dr. Smith's book on Lincoln. Ninian W. Edwards, his brother-in-law, reported Lincoln told him, "I have been reading a work of Dr. Smith on the evidences of Christianity, and have heard him preach and converse on the subject and am now convinced of the truth of the Christian religion."[16]

A few months after Mrs. Lincoln became a member of the First Presbyterian Church in 1852, Lincoln upon invitation of the session lectured on the Bible. Perhaps we have the outline of that address embedded in a letter Dr. Smith wrote to Herndon. His pastor reported Lincoln to have said about the Bible:

"It seems to me that nothing short of infinite wisdom could by any possibility have devised and given to man this excellent and perfect moral code. It is suited to men in all the conditions of life, and inculcates all the duties they owe to their Creator, to themselves, and to their fellow men."[17]

Sometime during this period Lincoln read Robert Chambers's *Vestiges of the Natural History of Creation,* first published in Edinburgh in 1844. Its aim was to reconcile the newly discovered materials in geology, paleontology, and biology with the Christian doctrine of creation. The book passed through many revisions, each time incorporating new scientific data. Herndon

86

described its influence upon Lincoln. "The treatise interested him greatly, and he was deeply impressed with the notion of the so-called 'universal law'—evolution; he did not greatly extend his researches, but by continual thinking in a single channel seemed to grow into a warm advocate of the new doctrine."[18]

In a letter, Herndon wrote that Lincoln subsequently read the sixth edition of *Vestiges* and as a result "adopted the progressive and development theory as taught more or less directly in that work. He despised speculation, especially in the metaphysical world. He was purely a practical man."[19] The significance of this is that Lincoln thought his way through to the acceptance of an evolutionary framework from a writing that was not anti-Christian but instead showed the living God at work in the processes described by science.

More of this liberal religious approach he could discover in the books of Theodore Parker, pressed upon him by Herndon, or in the collected works of William Ellery Channing which Jesse Fell presented to him "some eight or ten years prior to his death."[20]

Chapter 5

Lincoln had to shout to make himself heard above the shuffling crowd as it surged away from the House of Representatives in Springfield. From the vantage point of the stairway he announced that he would answer Judge Douglas's speech the next day. Douglas had just addressed a vast crowd gathered on October 3, 1854, for the Springfield Fair. He had boldly defended his role in the passage of the Kansas-Nebraska Act. His justification was the principle of popular sovereignty whereby the settlers would themselves determine whether or not to become slave states. He argued against his opponents that his stand was not a repeal of the Missouri Compromise and its subsequent reaffirmation in 1850, but a truly democratic extension of its very principles.

Douglas's Nebraska bill, Lincoln later said, "roused him as

nothing had before." It drew him away from the law at a time when "he had been losing interest in politics." A marked change, however, characterized Lincoln on his return to politics in 1854 from his virtual withdrawal from them in 1849. Then he had been the local boy who made good by hard work and pleasing personality, but above all by working with the Whig machine. When Lincoln returned to politics he still had the drive of ambition and the hunger for recognition, but these were not now paramount: they were held in check and ennobled by dedication to a cause. The authority of moral leadership is increasingly to be recognized in his speeches. In finding a cause that was bigger than himself Lincoln actually found himself.

His biographer, Benjamin Thomas, evaluates the new Lincoln: "The impact of a moral challenge, purging Lincoln of narrow partisanship and unsure purpose, is about to transform an honest, capable, but essentially self-centered small-town politican of self-developed but largely unsuspected talents into a statesman who will grow to world dimensions."[1]

Here also is the key to the religious development of Lincoln up to the time of the presidency. While the documents of this period offer little in the way of a personal statement of faith, they are vibrant with indignation over Douglas's indifference to the moral question of slavery. He was doubly disturbed when this moral indifference was offered as a calculated policy for political action. To state that Lincoln's opposition to slavery was rooted in his conception of morality is only, however, to give a part of the picture. His conception of morality itself was derived from religion. He would later say that without the revelation of the Bible man could not distinguish between right and wrong. Lincoln did not believe in an independent system of moral values. The good for Lincoln was ultimately anchored in the will of God, not subject to human likes or dislikes.

The motivating forces in his religious view of the world that shaped his moral decision on slavery are distinguishable in at least two directions. One was a theological understanding of the significance of work that was quarried from the Bible. "In the sweat of thy face shalt thou eat bread." This came increasingly to the fore in the later years of the presidency. The second was a passion for the fundamental equality of all men "in the sight of God" that Lincoln believed had been covenanted in the Declaration of Independence. That document had for him the force of revelation itself. It was this second point that he would affirm again and again in the classical debates with Douglas.

Far too many studies of Lincoln's religion, in their concentration upon personal piety, have neglected the deep, spiritual dynamic that underlay his attitude toward slavery. Lincoln's religion cannot be hermetically sealed off from his social, economic, and political attitudes. His political action, as revealed by his own words, was ultimately the social expression of an understanding of God and of man that demanded responsible activity. This is contrary to a widespread modern opinion that religion should be a separate interest or even hobby in life and should not be allowed to influence fields like politics.

No person as deeply immersed as Lincoln in the biblical

faith could possibly take such a view. His criticism of the churches of his day was that they neglected this fundamental love of God and of neighbor by too much introverted attention upon correctness in theological opinion. Prophetically Lincoln saw that concern for orthodoxy substituted for practical obedience.

This perspective in Lincoln must not be confused, however, with another view that the churches themselves should mix in politics. He took a dim view of preachers who used the pulpit for politics and said he preferred those who preached "the gospel." By this, however, he meant that the layman's task was to put this gospel to work not merely in individual piety, although certainly there, but also in responsible political activity. As a biblical believer Lincoln saw God dealing with men not merely as isolated individuals with capacities for piety but as men in social orders that are answerable to the Almighty.

Lincoln was very far from the modern heresy of believing that religion itself is a very good thing irrespective of its relation to everyday life. A Tennessee woman once sought a pardon for her husband, who was held prisoner in the Johnson's Island Camp, on the ground that her husband was a religious man. Lincoln granted the pardon but replied, "You say your husband is a religious man; tell him when you meet him, that I say I am not much of a judge of religion, but that, in my opinion, the religion that sets men to rebel and fight against their government, because, as they think, that government does not sufficiently help *some* men to eat their bread in the sweat of *other* men's faces, is not the sort of religion upon which people can get to heaven!"[2]

The religious substratum of Lincoln's attitude toward slavery needs to be highlighted today for still another reason. It is in danger of being wholly left out of the picture in the concentration of a number of recent studies on his political maneuvering and on the problems about the constitutionality of the issue. What is needed is to see the way in which the religious ground is expressed in the shifting political attitudes and strategies. The full picture requires all the components and not just selected ones.

On the fourth of October in a suffocating heat wave Lincoln, without coat and tie, stood up before a packed audience to answer Douglas. By invitation the judge sat before him in the front row. The report of this Springfield address appears in much-abbreviated form in the *Illinois Journal,* but the three-hour speech was fortunately repeated on October 15 in Peoria and recorded.

Lincoln argued that the founders of the Republic had had to accept the slavery that existed among them. In prohibiting slavery in the Northwest Territories, however, by the Ordinance of 1787 they adopted a principle of putting it in course of ultimate extinction. This principle of the non-extension of slavery to territories had, Lincoln argued, been consistently held. The Missouri Compromise of 1820 and its reaffirmation in 1850 resulted from a partial giving and taking on both sides.

Now, however, the Douglas Nebraska bill in effect destroyed the previous agreements by providing for squatter sovereignty under the high-sounding principle of democracy. "This *declared* indifference, but as I must think, covert *real zeal* for the spread of slavery, I can not but hate. I hate it because of the monstrous injustice of slavery itself. I hate it because it deprives our republican example of its just influence in the world . . ."[3] Because of the slavery issue, Americans were driven into war upon civil liberty and into contempt for the Declaration of Independence.

He wanted to assure the South that he was not prejudiced against them. The problem was national, not sectional. "They are just what we would be in their situation. If slavery did not now exist amongst them, they would not introduce it. If it did now exist amongst us, we should not instantly give it up. This I believe of the masses north and south."

If Lincoln had the power, he would not know how to deal with the existing situation. Probably he would free all the slaves and send them to Liberia. His own feelings would not allow him to make them politically and socially his equals. He wanted the South to know that he stood by their constitutional right to own slaves in the slave states and to have a fugitive slave law enforced. He was concerned only to prevent its spread. He wanted to keep it just where the Founding Fathers had placed it—in course of ultimate extinction "in God's good time."

His quarrel was with Douglas's interpretation of a great principle. "The doctrine of self-government is right—absolutely and eternally right—but it has no just application, as here attempted. Or perhaps I should rather say that whether it has such just application depends upon whether a negro is *not* or *is* a man. If he is *not* a man, why in that case, he who *is* a man may, as a matter of self-government, do just as he pleases with him. But if the negro *is* a man, is it not to that extent a total destruction of self-government, to say that he too shall not govern *him-*

94

self? When the white man governs himself that is self-government; but when he governs himself, and also governs *another* man, that is *more* than self-government—that is despotism. If the negro is a *man*, why then my ancient faith teaches me that 'all men are created equal'; and that there can be no moral right in connection with one man's making a slave of another.

"Judge Douglas frequently, with bitter irony and sarcasm, paraphrases our argument by saying, 'The white people of Nebraska are good enough to govern themselves, *but they are not good enough to govern a few miserable negroes!*'

"Well I doubt not that the people of Nebraska are, and will continue to be as good as the average of people elsewhere. I do not say the contrary. What I do say is, that no man is good enough to govern another man, *without that other's consent.* I say this is the leading principle—the sheet anchor of American republicanism. Our Declaration of Independence says:

" 'We hold these truths to be self evident: That all men are created equal; that they are endowed by their Creator with certain inalienable rights; that among these are life, liberty and the pursuit of happiness. That to secure these rights, governments are instituted among men, DERIVING THEIR JUST POWERS FROM THE CONSENT OF THE GOVERNED.' "

Later in the speech he said, "To deny these things is to deny our national axioms, or dogmas." Here is the key that unlocks Lincoln's fundamental attitude toward slavery. The axiom that all men are created equal had for him the force of religious dogma. Jefferson was Lincoln's mentor in political philosophy, but Lincoln's religious perspective was more concrete than Jefferson's. Lincoln went deeper than "self-evidence" for these

95

truths, even further than the somewhat deistic phrase "endowed by their Creator." For Lincoln the Creator was the living God of history, revealed in the Bible, Whose judgments were continuously written on the pages of history and recorded in the human conscience.

He drove the problem back to a view of human nature. "Slavery is founded in the selfishness of man's nature—opposition to it, in his love of justice. .... Repeal the Missouri Compromise . . . repeal all past history, you still can not repeal human nature." Then in the phraseology of the Bible he took a stand on bedrock: "It still will be the abundance of man's heart, that slavery extension is wrong; and out of the abundance of his heart, his mouth will continue to speak."

The proof that Lincoln understood the Declaration not merely as a national axiom but as a universal dogma is found in his Lewistown, Illinois, speech of August 17, 1858. It is a shame that this speech is so little known. Here the Declaration was specifically identified with the Genesis doctrine of man as created in the divine image. After quoting the same section of the Declaration that he had used in the Peoria speech, he went on to establish its theological foundation.

"This was their majestic interpretation of the economy of the Universe. This was their lofty, and wise, and noble understanding of the justice of the Creator to His creatures. Yes, gentlemen, to *all* His creatures, to the whole great family of man. In their enlightened belief, nothing stamped with the Divine image and likeness was sent into the world to be trodden on, and degraded, and imbruted by its fellows. They grasped not only the whole race of man then living, but they reached forward and seized

96

upon the farthest posterity. They erected a beacon to guide their children and their children's children, and the countless myriads who should inhabit the earth in other ages. Wise statesmen as they were, they knew the tendency of prosperity to breed tyrants, and so they established these great self-evident truths, that when in the distant future some man, some faction, some interest, should set up the doctrine that none but rich men, or none but white men, were entitled to life, liberty and the pursuit of happiness, their posterity might look up again to the Declaration of Independence and take courage to renew the battle which the fathers began—so that truth, and justice, and mercy, and all the humane and Christian virtues might not be extinguished from the land; so that no man would hereafter dare to limit and circumscribe the great principles on which the temple of liberty was being built."[4]

Lincoln's astute rival in the great debates of 1858 understood Lincoln's theological perspective on the slavery issue. Three times Douglas attacked Lincoln on just this point. At Ottawa, Douglas accused him of having "learned by heart Parson Lovejoy's catechism." He said that Lincoln "holds that the negro was born his equal and yours, and that he was endowed with equality by the Almighty, and that no human law can deprive him of these rights, which were guaranteed to him by the Supreme Ruler of the Universe."

In the seventh and last debate at Alton, Douglas summarized his stand with merciless clarity. "I care more for the great principle of self-government, the right of the people to rule, than I do for all the negroes in Christendom. [Cheers.] I would not endanger the perpetuity of this Union. I would not blot out

97

the great inalienable rights of white men for all the negroes that ever existed. [Renewed applause.]"

Judge Douglas had pointed out that because the Founding Fathers did not abolish slavery they understood "all men" in the Declaration to mean "white men." Lincoln repudiated this narrowed interpretation in his Chicago speech, strengthening the religious dimension in his view with Scripture.

"We had slavery among us, we could not get our Constitution unless we permitted them to remain in slavery, we could not secure the good we did secure if we grasped for more, and having by necessity submitted to that much, it does not destroy the principle that is the charter of our liberties. Let that charter stand as our standard.

"My friend has said to me that I am a poor hand to quote Scripture. I will try it again, however. It is said in one of the admonitions of the Lord, 'As your Father in Heaven is perfect, be ye also perfect.' The Savior, I suppose, did not expect that any human creature could be perfect as the Father in Heaven; but He said, 'As your Father in Heaven is perfect, be ye also perfect.' He set that up as a standard, and he who did most towards reaching that standard, attained the highest degree of moral perfection. So I say in relation to the principle that all men are created equal, let it be as nearly reached as we can."[5]

In this quotation Lincoln demonstrated his conviction that God's basic law of freedom in the creation of man was meant to be dynamically and progressively embodied in the positive legislation of states. T. Harry Williams, an editor of a selection of Lincoln's writings, establishes the religious orientation to Lincoln's theory of jurisprudence. "The doctrine of the existence of a supernatural fundamental law and the corollary that fundamental human law approximated the higher code was an important part of Lincoln's philosophy."[6]

In a speech at Cincinnati he warned those who justified slavery as a biblical ordinance that the institution mentioned in the Bible was *white* slavery, not *black* slavery. He doubted whether white slaveholders really wanted to defend their peculiar institution by a point that might make them the slaves of the next more powerful white man.

The Rutgers editors have followed Nicolay and Hay in assigning to the period of the great debates a remarkable fragment on pro-slavery theology. With the scorn of an Old Testament prophet Lincoln lays bare the taint of self-interest that corrupts man's judgments. His reference to Dr. Ross is probably to the pamphlet *Slavery as Ordained of God,* by the Rev. Frederick A. Ross of Alabama, published in 1857.

"Suppose it is true, that the negro is inferior to the white, in the gifts of nature; is it not the exact reverse justice that the white should, for that reason, take from the negro, any part of the little which has been given him? *'Give* to him that is needy' is the Christian rule of charity; but 'Take from him that is needy' is the rule of slavery.

"The sum of pro-slavery theology seems to be this: 'Slavery is not universally *right,* nor yet universally *wrong;* it is better for *some* people to be slaves; and, in such cases, it is the Will of God that they be such.'

"Certainly there is no contending against the Will of God; but still there is some difficulty in ascertaining, and applying it, to particular cases. For instance we will suppose the Rev.

Dr. Ross has a slave named Sambo, and the question is 'Is it the Will of God that Sambo shall remain a slave, or be set free?' The Almighty gives no audible answer to the question, and his revelation—the Bible—gives none, or, at most, none but such as admits of a squabble, as to its meaning. No one thinks of asking Sambo's opinion on it. So, at last, it comes to this, that *Dr. Ross* is to decide the question. And while he considers it, he sits in the shade, with gloves on his hands, and subsists on the bread that Sambo is earning in the burning sun. If he decides that God wills Sambo to continue a slave, he thereby retains his own comfortable position; but if he decides that God wills Sambo to be free, he thereby has to walk out of the shade, throw off his gloves, and delve for his own bread. Will Dr. Ross be actuated by that perfect impartiality, which has ever been considered most favorable to correct decisions?

"But, slavery is good for some people!!! As a *good* thing, slavery is strikingly peculiar, in this, that it is the only good thing which no man ever seeks the good of, for *himself*.

"Nonsense! Wolves devouring lambs, not because it is good for their own greedy maws, but because it is good for the lambs!!!"[7]

To his best friend Joshua Speed, a slaveholder, he had written straight from the shoulder: "It is hardly fair for you to assume, that I have no interest in a thing which has, and continually exercises, the power of making me miserable. You ought rather to appreciate how much the great body of the Northern people do crucify their feelings, in order to maintain their loyalty to the Constitution and the Union." Later in the same letter he related his feeling on slavery to the question of Speed about his political affiliation.

"I am not a Know-Nothing. That is certain. How could I be? How can any one who abhors the oppression of negroes, be in favor of degrading classes of white people? Our progress in degeneracy appears to me to be pretty rapid. As a nation, we began by declaring that *'all men are created equal.'* We now practically read it 'all men are created equal, *except negroes.'* When the Know-Nothings get control it will read 'all men are created equal, except negroes, *and foreigners, and Catholics.'* When it comes to this I should prefer emigrating to some country where they make no pretence of loving liberty—to Russia, for instance, where despotism can be taken pure, and without the base alloy of hypocrisy."[8]

About the same time he wrote to George Robertson, professor of law at Transylvania College, confessing that he could not see how the problem of slavery, the basic self-contradiction of American freedom, could be solved. He appealed beyond human measures to the God Who directs history. "Our political problem now is 'Can we, as a nation, continue together *permanently—forever*—half slave, and half free?' The problem is too mighty for me. May God, in his mercy, superintend the solution."[9]

In the Second Inaugural he would show how God had dealt with this cancer in the nation. In the presidential years he could move forward on the slavery issue only when he had first resolved the conflict between his oath to uphold the Constitution with its entrenched institution of slavery and the practical war measures which he felt obliged to take in order to preserve and then restore the Union. Behind this dramatic struggle, however, this theological orientation on slavery continually exerted pressure on him.

He believed slavery was a moral evil; he believed it was against the constitution of the universe; he believed it was a mocking of the God Who had created the Negro in His own image as He had all men. He believed that the injustice of slavery invited the wrath of God.

He expressed this last conviction strongly at Columbus, Ohio, on September 16, 1859, in a contrast he drew between Jefferson and Douglas: ". . . but that man did not take exactly this view of the insignificance of the element of slavery which our friend Judge Douglas does. In contemplation of this thing, we all know he was led to exclaim, 'I tremble for my country when I remember that God is just!' We know how he looked upon it when he thus expressed himself. There was danger to this country—danger of the avenging justice of God in that little unimportant popular sovereignty question of Judge Douglas. He supposed there was a question of God's eternal justice wrapped up in the enslaving of any race of men, or any man, and that those who did so braved the arm of Jehovah—that when a nation thus dared the Almighty every friend of that nation had cause to dread His wrath. Choose ye between Jefferson and Douglas as to what is the true view of this element among us."[10]

The biblical coloration of this motivating conviction would become even stronger in his many expositions of the text: "In the sweat of thy face, thou shalt eat bread." To a degree he anticipated this later position in a fragment on free labor, probably from his Cincinnati speech of September 1859. "As labor is the common *burthen* of our race, so the effort of *some* to shift their share of the burthen on to the shoulders of *others,* is the great, durable, curse of the race. Originally a curse for transgression upon the whole race, when, as by slavery, it is concentrated on a part only, it becomes the double-refined curse of God upon his creatures."[11]

Lincoln's use of the titles "Lord" and "Savior" in the passages quoted and in other references during this late Springfield period is about as far as the direct evidence goes for any distinctly Christian orientation at this time. It is important, however, not to underestimate the significance of these ascriptions. In his many quotations of Christ's words Lincoln does not use them as the sayings of "the great teacher" in a humanist sense but as the teaching of one who is "the Lord" and "the Savior" in an implicitly Christological sense.

There are, moreover, some important comments by friends of his that, if evaluated with caution, help to give more background to his understanding of Christ as "the Savior" and "the Lord." There is a high probability in this evidence because it builds with some consistency on the statement of Mentor Graham, previously quoted, that Lincoln wrote an essay about 1833 on predestinated universal salvation in criticism of the orthodox doctrine of endless punishment.

It is also consistent with the evidence that in 1850 Lincoln, through the reading of his pastor's *The Christian's Defense* and his own wrestling with the problem, became convinced intellectually of the validity of the biblical revelation. This would not have meant that Lincoln accepted the Calvinistic theology of his clergyman friend. Lincoln's conviction that God would restore the whole of creation as the outcome of Christ's Atonement would have been in itself a bar to membership in the Springfield church he attended. His often expressed impatience with creedal formularies as a condition for church membership surely reflects the struggle between his independent analysis of biblical teaching and the pressures upon him to conform to conventional denominationalism. The weight of this evidence is, moreover, considerably strengthened when the Jesse Fell statement, often thought to be impossible of reconciliation with those of Isaac Cogdal and Jonathan Harnett, is seen to be much less of a problem than supposed.

Isaac Cogdal, who had known Lincoln from the time of the New Salem period, recalled a discussion on religion in Lincoln's office in 1859. ". . . Herndon was in the office at the time. Lincoln expressed himself in about these words: He did not nor could not believe in the endless punishment of any one of the human race. He understood punishment for sin to be a Bible doctrine; that the punishment was parental in its object, aim, and design, and intended for the good of the offender; hence it must cease when justice is satisfied. He added that all that was lost by the transgression of Adam was made good by the atonement: all that was lost by the fall was made good by the sacrifice, and he added this remark, that punishment being a 'provision of the gospel system, he was not sure but the world would be better off if a little more punishment was preached by our ministers, and not so much pardon of sin.' "[12]

This last comment has all the earmarks of an authentic

Lincoln utterance. It shows the independence with which he handled biblical evidence in reaching a conclusion at odds with current preaching practice. His basic acceptance of "the provisions of the gospel system" gave him this leverage against popular religion. The prophetic note of a God of mercy Who punishes the sins of men in the judgments of history with a view to reformation would become a dominant theme in his later religious utterances, especially in his presidential proclamations.

Here Lincoln saw much more clearly than most parsons of his day that there is an unbiblical preaching of pardon for sin that, by extricating the individual man from his historical and social setting, gives him illusions about punishment in this world and the next. Lincoln understood the gospel to mean the salvation of all men in both a this-worldly and a next-worldly framework. Many ministers had reduced Christianity to a message of escape for individuals from punishment in the next world. Lincoln's emphasis upon sacrifice as a key to "the economy of the universe" would be immeasurably deepened in the crucible of the war years.

The second statement was one dictated by Jonathan Harnett of Pleasant Plains, describing a theological discussion in 1858 in Lincoln's office. "Lincoln covered more ground in a few words than he could in a week, and closed up with the restitution of all things to God, as the doctrine taught in the scriptures, and if anyone was left in doubt in regard to his belief in the atonement of Christ and the final salvation of all men, he removed those doubts in a few questions he answered and propounded to others. After expressing himself, some one or two took exceptions to his position, and he asked a few questions that cornered his interrogators and left no room to doubt or question his soundness on the atonement of Christ, and salvation finally of all men. He did not pretend to know just when that event would be consummated, but that it would be the ultimate result, that Christ must reign supreme, high over all, The Saviour of all; and the supreme Ruler, he could not be with one out of the fold; all must come in, with his understanding of the doctrine taught in the scriptures."[13]

The Harnett dictation strengthens the testimony to Lincoln's belief in Christ as ultimately the Savior of all and points to that fifteenth chapter of I Corinthians previously discussed in connection with Mentor Graham's statement. This was clearly the biblical locus for Lincoln's arguments on this theme.

The Jesse Fell statement is better known than the two just quoted chiefly because it was written for Colonel Ward Lamon's *Life of Abraham Lincoln* and was reprinted by Herndon in his biography. The problem with this statement is that, taken in isolation from other evidence, it tends to suggest to the reader more than it actually says. If this were the sole statement on Lincoln's religion it might be concluded that Lincoln wholly rejected Christianity for a practical belief "summed up . . . in these two propositions: the Fatherhood of God, and the brotherhood of man."

Fell was a pioneer in introducing the liberal Christianity of William Ellery Channing into Illinois, being responsible for establishing a Unitarian Church in Bloomington shortly after 1859. Lincoln's habit of saying that he would join a church that inscribed over its altars as a condition of membership "the

Savior's summary of the Gospel" obviously opened an area of discussion between Lincoln and Fell, but there was still a major difference between the two. Lincoln adopted a liberal attitude that brought him into disagreement with the "orthodox" religion on such points as limited atonement and eternal punishment. But it was on the very anvil of a belief in Christ as atoner and God as punisher for purposes of reformation that he hammered out his criticism. In other words, Lincoln took a liberal attitude toward biblical orthodoxy as he understood it.

Fell, on the other hand, went beyond the liberal attitude of Lincoln and began to substitute for biblical orthodoxy a set of distinctly liberal dogmas such as the fatherhood of God and the brotherhood of man. Fell said later that had the circumstances of his life been different he would have wanted to be a Unitarian minister. Channing's Unitarianism, moreover, was of the "high" variety. It was theistic and not humanist. It had a Christology of its own.

Fell says of Lincoln's religion in the Springfield period: "whilst he held many opinions in common with the great mass of Christian believers, he did not believe in what are regarded as the orthodox or evangelical views of Christianity.

"On the innate depravity of man, the character and office of the great head of the Church, the Atonement, the infallibility of the written revelation, the performance of miracles, the nature and design of present and future rewards and punishments (as they are popularly called) and many other subjects, he held opinions utterly at variance with what are usually taught in the Church."[14]

Here is where the unwary reader may read more out of the

passage than Fell meant to put in. Fell is not saying that Lincoln did not believe *at all* in Christ as Atoner nor that Lincoln did not *at all* accept the belief that God punishes. He says that *on* these subjects his views were "utterly at variance" with current orthodoxy. The word "utterly" is perhaps too strong in its suggestions, but it is still true in perspective. The Calvinist theology of that day stressed an atonement by Christ limited to those predestined to be saved. The fate of unbelievers in eternal flames was a commonplace of the preacher of that period.

Fell completed the substance of his description as follows: "He fully believed in a superintending and overruling Providence that guides and controls the operations of the world, but maintained that law and order, not their violation or suspension, are the appointed means by which this Providence is exercised." The theme of God's providential guidance would be Lincoln's clue to interpreting religiously the meaning of the nation's history in the presidential years.

The trouble with so many studies of Lincoln's religion is that they soon bog down in the clash of other people's testimony about his belief. It is therefore a relief to turn from the Cogdal, Harnett, and Fell statements to an exciting new source revealed in 1957 with the discovery of a devotional book first published in 1852 and inscribed with Lincoln's name. In an introduction to the reprinting of *The Believer's Daily Treasure; or, Texts of Scripture Arranged for Every Day in the Year*, Sandburg suggests that either the book was given to Lincoln by a person for whom he cared or that he held the book itself in high regard, for he seldom wrote his name, even for purposes of identification, in his own books.

It was of course in 1852 that his wife joined the First Presbyterian Church and that he attended some of the inquirers' sessions in addition to their regular attendance at Sunday worship. Possibly his wife gave him this tiny book to carry with him on the judicial circuit. Possibly his pastor gave him this biblical devotional. It is just the book that could have fed Lincoln's soul. Completely free of denominational dogmas, it presents the evangelical core of the Bible as a practical guide to everyday life.

Its many references from the Psalms may throw light on a remark Lincoln later made to a nurse in the White House: "They are the best, for I find in them something for every day in the week."[15] Although we do not have any statement of Lincoln's as to how much or little he used this devotional manual, there may well have been considerable influence. The following quotations have been selected to give the flavor of the book and to show some parallelism with the great religious themes of his later state papers.[16]

"Believer's Evidences
FEBRUARY 27 — LOVE TO ENEMIES

Love ye your enemies, and do good, and lend, hoping for nothing again; and your reward shall be great, and ye shall be the children of the Highest: for he is kind unto the unthankful and to the evil.   Luke 6:3

Lord, shall thy bright example shine
In vain before my eyes?
Give me a soul akin to thine,
To love my enemies.

Duties of the Believer — in the Church
MAY 13 — MUTUAL CANDOUR

Judge not, that ye be not judged. Why beholdest thou the mote that is in thy brother's eye, but considerest not the beam that is in thine own eye?   Matt. 7:1,3

Make us by thy transforming grace,
Great Saviour, daily more like thee
Thy fair example may we trace,
To teach us what we ought to be.

Joys of the Believer
JULY 20 — TRIBULATION A SOURCE OF JOY

We glory in tribulation: knowing that tribulation worketh patience; and patience, experience; and experience, hope. Rom. 5:3,4."

When the balloting came for the Illinois legislature which would itself elect the United States senator, the Republican candidates received four thousand more votes than their opponents. An unrepresentative system of apportionment, however, made possible the election of Douglas. Lincoln had lost the senatorship. Again he turned to his much-neglected law practice. He did not of course realize that, while he could not be senator in 1859, he would, chiefly by the fame of these debates, become the President in 1861.

To his personal friend and physician he wrote, "I am glad I made the late race. It gave me a hearing on the great and durable question of the age, which I could have had in no other way; and though I now sink out of view, and shall be forgotten, I believe I have made some marks which will tell for the cause of civil liberty long after I am gone."[17]

Contrary to his prophecy, he did not sink out of view. In the excitement leading up to Lincoln's nomination at Chicago and even in the presidential campaign itself, since by the conventions of that day candidates did not campaign for themselves, there is little in Lincoln's own words that throws light on his continuing religious development. Since the slavery theme has been chosen to illustrate the theological rootage of Lincoln's attitude on the great question of his age it will be well to note a few developments here. The debates with Douglas convinced Lincoln that he needed to do basic research on the attitude of the Founding Fathers to "the peculiar institution." Long hours were spent poring over materials in the Illinois State Library and in digesting Elliot's *Debates on the Federal Constitution.* The fruit of this scholarly research strengthened the Cooper Union address in New York in February 1860. This speech made him better known in the East.

A new incisiveness and a rhetoric strengthened by homespun but graphic illustrations show his intellectual growth in this period. At Hartford, Connecticut, on March 5, 1860, he stated with a succinctness never reached in his debates with Douglas the Republican opposition to the spread of slavery.

"For instance, out in the street, or in the field, or on the prairie I find a rattlesnake. I take a stake and kill him. Everybody would applaud the act and say I did right. But suppose the snake was in a bed when children were sleeping. Would I do right to strike him there? I might hurt the children; or I might not kill, but only arouse and exasperate the snake, and he might bite the children. Thus, by meddling with him here, I would do more hurt than good. Slavery is like this. We dare not strike at it where it is. The manner in which our Constitution is framed constrains us from making war upon it where it already exists. The question that we now have to deal with is, 'Shall we be acting right to take this snake and carry it to a bed where there are children?' The Republican party insists upon keeping it out of the bed."[18]

At New Haven he gave a humorous twist to his point that the defense of slavery was vitiated by ideological taint. His story parallels his earlier one about Dr. Ross, Sambo, and pro-slavery theology.

"The slaveholder does not like to be considered a mean fellow for holding that species of property, and hence he has to struggle within himself and sets about arguing himself into the belief that slavery is right. The property influences his mind. The dissenting minister, who argued some theological point with one of the established church, was always met with the reply, 'I can't see it so.' He opened the Bible, and pointed him to a passage, but the orthodox minister replied, 'I can't see it so.' Then he showed him a single word—'Can you see that?' 'Yes, I see it,' was the reply. The dissenter laid a guinea over the word and asked, 'Do you see it now?' [Great laughter.]

So here. Whether the owners of this species of property do really see it as it is, it is not for me to say, but if they do, they see it as it is through 2,000,000,000 of dollars, and that is a pretty thick coating. [Laughter.]"[19]

He felt keenly the inertia and resistance of the clergy on the moral issue of slavery. Shortly before the election in October 1860 he and Newton Bateman thumbed through a list of how Springfield residents were proposing to vote. When he concluded that twenty out of twenty-three ministers would vote against him, he asked sadly how it could be possible for men with the Bible in their hands to support candidates who were in effect pro-slavery.

Most of the incidents and themes in Lincoln's religious development in the Springfield period are summed up in his moving Farewell Address. Here was his deep sense of belonging to the people and the sadness of leaving friends. He recalled the birth of his children and the death of one of them. Seven states were already in secession and many federal forts and arsenals had been seized in the South. Lincoln spoke in sober tones of the responsibility placed upon him, the great and deepening theme of the years to come. Here was the foreboding that he might not return, that premonition that would later be expressed as a doubt that he himself would outlive the national conflict.

But if man by himself is weak God is all-powerful. If the "Doctrine of Necessity" once may have had the impersonal cast of determinism upon it, it had now been replaced by a faith in the God Who is personally and intimately concerned for every man and Who providentially brings to pass His designs for good in man's history. He commended his friends to God's care and asked for their prayers for him. "Doctor," said Lincoln to his friend and pastor at their last meeting before the departure, "I wish to be remembered in the prayers of yourself and our church members."

In the cold drizzle of that February day, with an expression of tragic sadness on his face, Lincoln spoke from the platform of the special train. The stubby locomotive tested its steam and the people peered upward from under their sheltering umbrellas.

"My friends—No one, not in my situation, can appreciate my feeling of sadness at this parting. To this place, and the kindness of these people, I owe everything. Here I have lived a quarter of a century, and have passed from a young to an old man. Here my children have been born, and one is buried. I now leave, not knowing when, or whether ever, I may return, with a task before me greater than that which rested upon Washington. Without the assistance of that Divine Being who ever attended him, I cannot succeed. With that assistance, I cannot fail. Trusting in Him who can go with me, and remain with you, and be everywhere for good, let us confidently hope that all will yet be well. To His care commending you, as I hope in your prayers you will commend me, I bid you an affectionate farewell."[20]

"An Humble Instrument in the Hands of the Almighty"

Chapter 6

The acceleration in Lincoln's religious development that came with his assuming the burdens of the presidency in a time of civil conflict may be traced to two sources. The first was the personal anguish of the death of friends and the tragic loss of his beloved Willie. The second was the suffering and pain that tore at the nation's life in crisis after crisis and cried aloud for some interpretation. The erosion of these forces may be traced in the deepening facial lines of almost every subsequent photograph of Lincoln. The first pressure turned Lincoln toward a deeper piety than he had known before. The second inspired him to probe beneath the seeming irrationality of events for a prophetic understanding of the nation's history. The first was clearly reflected in the Farewell Address at Springfield and the second began to find expression in the First Inaugural.

In this conciliating speech designed to allay Southern fears Lincoln argued for the perpetuity of the Union. The Union preceded even the adoption of the Constitution, which was itself established "to form a more perfect Union." Government must proceed by majority rule. The unwillingness of a minority to accept majority rule was the very principle of anarchy and despotism since a secession from the Union would itself be disrupted within a few years by the momentum of dissent. The facts of geography, moreover, made any separation unviable. "They cannot but remain face to face; and intercourse, either amicable or hostile, must continue between them. . . . Can aliens make treaties easier than friends can make laws? . . . Suppose you go to war, you cannot fight always; and when, after much loss on both sides, and no gain on either, you cease fighting, the identical old questions, as to terms of intercourse are again upon you."

Lincoln then expressed his conviction of the essential rightness and wisdom of the people if allowed time to register their verdict. His confidence in the people had its roots in religious reality and its presupposition in God. It was not the secular theory that the will of the people constituted right. That is the principle of mobocracy. *Vox populi, vox dei* meant for Lincoln that, if not thwarted by man's rebellion, God so guided the consciences of men in history that the people's verdict was properly their response to His guidance. Even the qualification in this last sentence, "if not thwarted by man's rebellion," needs further modification, for Lincoln held that God was constantly overruling those designs which were at cross-purposes with His own.

This theme was no isolated one for Lincoln. He had expressed it again and again on that circuitous train journey from Spring-field to Washington. In Buffalo he gave it this form: "For the ability to perform it, I must trust in that Supreme Being who has never forsaken this favored land, through the instrumen-tality of this great and intelligent people."[1] In Trenton he told the New Jersey senators what Weems's *Life of Washington* had meant to him as a boy. The Revolutionary fathers had struggled for more than just national independence. It was "something that held out a great promise to all the people of the world to all time to come" and Lincoln would be most happy if he might "be an humble instrument in the hands of the Al-mighty, and of this, his almost chosen people, for perpetuating the object of that great struggle."[2] The inspired phrase, "his almost chosen people," will be discussed more fully in Chap-ter 8.

For Lincoln, confidence in the rightness of democratic process had as its presupposition faith in the history-molding God of justice and mercy. Not a pious addendum or a rhetorical tail-piece, Lincoln's faith in the Almighty Ruler of nations provided the dynamic and justification for a high confidence in the essen-tial integrity of the people. He would spell out this theme in many ways in the years ahead.

"Why should there not be a patient confidence in the ultimate justice of the people? Is there any better, or equal hope, in the world? In our present differences, is either party without faith of being in the right? If the Almighty Ruler of nations, with his eternal truth and justice, be on your side of the North, or on yours of the South, that truth, and that justice, will surely prevail, by the judgment of this great tribunal, the American people."

Lincoln had earlier in the speech defined "the substantial dispute" as between the section that "believes slavery is *right*, and ought to be extended" and the other that "believes it is *wrong*, and ought not to be extended." He then took the seeming moral impasse between the contestants and placed it beyond the merely moral. Since each party believed it was right and shared a common faith in the God Who ruled the nations he appealed to each to accept God's verdict of rightness which, if allowed expression in the maintenance of the Union, would sooner or later be made evident by "the judgment of this great tribunal, the American people."

Then, spelling out the same conviction in a slightly different way, he counseled the South not to take precipitate action. If they who were dissatisfied were in the right, it was clear that God Himself would so guide the nation that adjustments would be made. This awareness sprang not from any conviction of the inherent virtue of one side in the controversy offering relief to dissatisfied opponents, a self-righteous condescension likely to exacerbate controversy, but from the perspective of the God of truth and justice Who would overrule both sides. From this religious point of vantage the bitter strife between two sides equally convinced of their own integrity and virtue was moderated by an appeal to a higher court without, however, loss of responsibility.

"Intelligence, patriotism, Christianity, and a firm reliance on Him, who has never yet forsaken this favored land, are still competent to adjust, in the best way, all our present difficulty."

Then, reworking Seward's somewhat prosaic suggestions for a final paragraph with the alchemy of his touch, Lincoln appealed to the shared memories of the past. In the coming years he would as no other President has ever done deepen for the American people the "mystic chords of memory" that make them a community.

"I am loth to close. We are not enemies, but friends. We must not be enemies. Though passion may have strained, it must not break our bonds of affection. The mystic chords of memory, stretching from every battlefield, and patriot grave, to every living heart and hearthstone, all over this broad land, will yet swell the chorus of the Union, when again touched, as surely they will be, by the better angels of our nature."[3]

The hope expressed in the First Inaugural that there would be no violence was shattered by the hostilities at Fort Sumter within a little more than a month. Virginia seceded and the war was on in earnest. Then toward the end of July came the humiliating disaster at Bull Run. In response to a resolution of both Houses of Congress, Lincoln appointed a national fast day in a proclamation signed by Seward as Secretary of State and by himself.

The themes of this remarkable document are a further development of his prophetic understanding of the nation's history. They crowd so fast one upon the other that the reader often fails to appreciate their amazing scope. Governments must acknowledge the lordship of God over their life. They must contritely confess their faults "as a nation and as individuals." The present conflict was the chastisement of God. Men would do well "to recognize the hand of God in this terrible visitation."

Just how men should interpret this "visitation" was not spelled out. Much of Lincoln's subsequent meditation would center around this idea until a full and clear answer would be given in the Second Inaugural. God guided the fathers into the pathway of civil and religious liberty. Prayer was offered for the restoration of the Union in "the . . . conviction that the fear of the Lord is the beginning of wisdom."

The style of Lincoln's proclamations differs, naturally, from that of his speeches. Daniel Dodge, in his *Abraham Lincoln: Master of Words*, suggested the influence of the Book of Common Prayer through Seward, who was an Episcopalian. The frequent repetition of the same idea by the use of words in pairs ("fit and becoming") is a characteristic of the liturgical rhythm of the Prayer Book, but it is also typical legal style in which the conjunction of synonyms gives greater precision in meaning. While Seward's influence may well be present, the ideas expressed are rooted in the biblical substratum of Lincoln's faith. The proclamations provide much of the background for understanding the Second Inaugural and are links in a chain leading up to it. Passing far beyond the bare language of the congressional resolution, which was a somewhat impenitent request for protection, Lincoln set the whole matter in a biblical frame of reference.

"And whereas it is fit and becoming in all people, at all times, to acknowledge and revere the Supreme Government of God; to bow in humble submission to His chastisements; to confess and deplore their sins and transgressions in the full conviction that the fear of the Lord is the beginning of wisdom; and to pray, with all fervency and contrition, for the pardon of their past offenses, and for a blessing upon their present and prospective action:

"And whereas, when our own beloved Country, once, by the blessing of God, united, prosperous and happy, is now afflicted with faction and civil war, it is peculiarly fit for us to recognize the hand of God in this terrible visitation, and in sorrowful remembrance of our own faults and crimes as a nation and as individuals, to humble ourselves before Him, and to pray for His mercy,—to pray that we may be spared further punishment, though most justly deserved; that our arms may be blessed and made effectual for the re-establishment of law, order and peace, throughout the wide extent of our country; and that the inestimable boon of civil and religious liberty, earned under His guidance and blessing, by the labors and sufferings of our fathers, may be restored in all its original excellence . . ."[4]

The harsh reality of death had always troubled Lincoln. He had known its coldness when as a lad of nine his mother breathed no more in the rude Indiana cabin. Then his sister had died. Still later their beloved Eddie was buried. Now with the outbreak of war Lincoln would feel the presence of death on an unprecedented scale. Elmer Ellsworth, his friend and former law student, was shot in the occupation of Alexandria and became one of the first casualties of the war. Lincoln wept at his funeral, held in the White House, and wrote a note of consolation to the boy's parents. "In the untimely loss of your noble son, our affliction here, is scarcely less than your own. . . . May God give you that consolation which is beyond all earthly power."[5]

This faith in God's healing power in bereavement would be critically tested when their son Willie fell dangerously ill early in 1862. After four or five final days of suffering and delirium, with the father sharing the night watch, the lad died on February 20. Although Tad was also gravely ill and not for a time expected to recover, Mrs. Lincoln removed herself from the sick child and took to her bed in grief. Friends worried for the President, so utterly crushed did he appear, but within two days of the funeral he called a cabinet meeting and carried on with the business of state.

Mrs. Rebecca Pomeroy, from Chelsea, Massachusetts, acted as special nurse for Willie and Tad. She spoke to Lincoln about the prayers of Christians all over the land for him in his bitter loss. "I am glad to hear that," she reported his words. "I want them to pray for me. I need their prayers. I will try to go to God with my sorrows. . . . I wish I had that childlike faith you speak of, and I trust He will give it to me. I had a good Christian mother, and her prayers have followed me thus far through life."[8]

Ida Tarbell describes the impact of this blow upon Lincoln. "There is ample evidence that in this crushing grief the President sought earnestly to find what consolation the Christian religion might have for him. It was the first experience of his life, so far as we know, which drove him to look outside of his own mind and heart for help to endure a personal grief. It was the first time in his life when he had not been sufficient for his own experience. Religion up to this time had been an intellectual interest. . . . From this time on he was seen often with the Bible in his hand, and he is known to have prayed frequently. His personal relation to God occupied his mind much."[7]

In his *Six Months at the White House* the painter Carpenter tells of a visit by the Rev. Francis Vinton of Trinity Church, New York, to the grief-stricken father. "Your son is *alive,* in Paradise," said Dr. Vinton, whom Mrs. Lincoln had asked to call. "Do you remember that passage in the Gospels: 'God is not the God of the *dead* but of the living, for *all* live unto him'?" Lincoln had a discussion with the rector and asked that his sermon on the subject of eternal life be sent to him. Carpenter relates that Lincoln read the sermon many times, having a copy made for his own use. "Through a member of the family, I have been informed that Mr. Lincoln's views in relation to spiritual things seemed changed from that hour."[8]

The flowering of this richer faith and Lincoln's deep human sympathy were expressed in his famous letter to the widow Bixby. Lincoln had been told that five of her sons had died in battle. The correct number was actually two. Its dominating thought is the Gettysburg speech in microcosm, personal loss sacrificially related to the preservation of freedom. Sandburg has called it "a piece of the American Bible . . . blood-color syllables of a sacred music."

"I feel how weak and fruitless must be any words of mine which should attempt to beguile you from the grief of a loss so overwhelming. But I cannot refrain from tendering to you the consolation that may be found in the thanks of the Republic they died to save. I pray that our Heavenly Father may assuage the anguish of your bereavement, and leave you only the cherished memory of the loved and lost, and the solemn pride that must be yours, to have laid so costly a sacrifice upon the altar of Freedom."[9]

Accompanying his deepened appreciation of the reality of eternal life came increased attention to prayer. Mrs. Lincoln is reported to have said that the morning of the ceremony of the inauguration Lincoln read the conclusion of the address to the family and then, when they had withdrawn from the room, prayed audibly for strength and guidance.[10]

In a letter, Noah Brooks wrote of Lincoln: "He said that after he went to the White House, he kept up the habit of daily prayer. Sometimes it was only ten words, but those ten words he had."[11]

John Nicolay, one of his secretaries, reported: "Mr. Lincoln was a praying man. I know that to be a fact and I have heard him request people to pray for him, which he would never have done had he not believed that prayer is answered. . . . I have heard him say that he prayed."[12]

For Lincoln the purpose of prayer was not to get God to do man's bidding but to place man where he might come to see God's purposes and to experience the strength of relying on the everlasting arms. A graphic picture of this resort to prayer is given by General James Rusling, who stood with the President in a Washington hospital at the bedside of General Sickles. The incident is doubly attested and has, moreover, the same authentic ring in the idiom about "a solemn vow to Almighty God" that had earlier marked his approach to emancipating the slaves. General Sickles had been wounded at Gettysburg and was recovering from a leg amputation.

"In reply to a question from General Sickles whether or not

the President was anxious about the battle at Gettysburg, Lincoln gravely said, 'No, I was not; some of my Cabinet and many others in Washington were, but I had no fears.' General Sickles inquired how this was, and seemed curious about it. Mr. Lincoln hesitated, but finally replied: 'Well, I will tell you how it was. In the pinch of the campaign up there, when everybody seemed panic-stricken, and nobody could tell what was going to happen, oppressed by the gravity of our affairs, I went to my room one day, and I locked the door, and got down on my knees before Almighty God, and prayed to Him mightily for victory at Gettysburg. I told Him that this was His war, and our cause His cause, but we couldn't stand another Fredericksburg or Chancellorsville. And I then and there made a solemn vow to Almighty God, that if He would stand by our boys at Gettysburg, I would stand by Him. And He *did* stand by your boys, and I *will* stand by Him. And after that (I don't know how it was, and I can't explain it), soon a sweet comfort crept into my soul that God Almighty had taken the whole business into his own hands and that things would go all right at Gettysburg. And that is why I had no fears about you."[13]

Prayer became increasingly a resource of strength to him. He began to speak more openly and in an unembarrassed way about it. This was in distinction to an earlier stage when he had maintained a wall of reserve about his religion and had chosen very carefully the men with whom he discussed it. To his newspaper friend Noah Brooks he once remarked: "I have been driven many times upon my knees by the overwhelming conviction that I had nowhere else to go."[14]

In the light of this evidence and of much more like it the popular image about Lincoln in the White House as a man of prayer is shown to have a solid basis in fact. This facet of Lincoln's religion has been graphically portrayed by Herbert S. Houck in his statue in the Washington Cathedral of Lincoln kneeling at prayer.

The relations of Lincoln as President with the clergy and churches of the country are fully detailed by Edgar DeWitt Jones in *Lincoln and the Preachers*. Here only those incidents will be described that throw light upon Lincoln's own faith or perhaps explain why he never became a church member. The pastor of the New York Avenue Presbyterian Church, Dr. Phineas D. Gurley, was, like his Springfield pastor, a Presbyterian of the Old School. Lincoln once told him that he could not perhaps accept all the doctrines in the Confession of Faith, but "if all that I am asked to respond to is what our Lord said were the two great commandments, to love the Lord thy God with all thy heart and mind and soul and strength, and my neighbor as myself, why, I aim to do that."

The Lincolns rented the eighth pew from the pulpit in Dr. Gurley's church and attended with regularity, their children sometimes accompanying them. Occasionally Lincoln went to the midweek prayer meeting. He must have gone often enough to make necessary the expedient of having him sit alone in the pastor's room, from which he could hear but not be seen by the congregation. This arrangement made it difficult for the curious to ruin the effect of the service and saved the President from their importunities afterward.

Delegations of churchmen brought him resolutions on the

war and on slavery. Some complained of the suspected heresies of men appointed as military chaplains. He listened with attention to them all, not hesitating at times to lecture those who lectured him.

To a committee of the Reformed Presbyterian Synod that petitioned him for emancipation he replied that their difference with him was not over the moral issue of slavery but over the best means to get rid of it. "Were an individual asked whether he would wish to have a wen on his neck, he could not hesitate as to the reply; but were it asked whether a man who has such a wen should at once be relieved of it by the application of the surgeon's knife, there might be diversity of opinion, perhaps the man might bleed to death, as the result of such an operation.

"Feeling deeply my responsibility to my country and to that God to whom we all owe allegiance, I assure you I will try to do my best, and so may God help me."[15]

Asked by the general superintendent of the Christian Commission to preside at a Washington's Birthday mass meeting in the House of Representatives in 1863, Lincoln declined, but approved its "worthy objects." His response, however, carried far beyond the conventional terms of the invitation, which had suggested in effect that the public meetings in other cities had served "to check distrust and disloyalty and to restore confidence and support to the Government."

The President replied in the spirit of the New Testament, "Whatever shall tend to turn our thoughts from the unreasoning, and uncharitable passions, prejudices, and jealousies incident to a great national trouble, such as ours, and to fix them upon the vast and long-enduring consequences, for weal, or for woe, which are to result from the struggle; and especially, to strengthen our reliance on the Supreme Being, for the final triumph of the right, can not but be well for us all."[16]

A Southern newspaper gave wide publicity to one of Lincoln's encounters with a clergyman in a delegation. The minister said he hoped "the Lord was on our side." When Lincoln rejoined, "I don't agree with you," the mouths of all were stopped. The President made it clearer. "I am not at all concerned about that, for I know that the Lord is *always* on the side of the *right*. But it is my constant anxiety and prayer that *I* and *this nation* should be on the Lord's side."[17]

One of the delegations drew from him the statement that he wished he were a more devout man. It is all of a piece with what he had told Generals Rusling and Sickles. It came shortly before his Gettysburg Address. This whole period was a time of greater consecration for Lincoln. His pastor Dr. Gurley had introduced the Baltimore Presbyterian Synod to the President and their moderator had offered their "respects" to him. "I was early brought to a living reflection," he replied, "that nothing in my power whatever, in others to rely upon, would succeed without the direct assistance of the Almighty, but all must fail. I have often wished that I was a more devout man than I am. Nevertheless, amid the greatest difficulties of my Administration, when I could not see any other resort, I would place my whole reliance in God, knowing that all would go well, and that He would decide for the right."[18]

Some of the delegations must have sorely tried his patience. Carpenter tells of an anti-slavery group from New York headed by a somewhat pompous and cocksure clergyman. "Well, gentlemen," said Lincoln in a deflating tone, "it is not often one is favored with a delegation *direct* from the Almighty." To another clergyman who on gaining admittance to his office said that he had merely called to pay his respects, Lincoln relaxed and said: "I am very glad to see you indeed. I thought you had come to preach to me!"

To the delegation that protested the choice of "unorthodox" chaplains by the regiments, Lincoln told the story of the little colored boy who was asked what he was making out of mud. The boy showed his questioner the little church building, the pews, and the pulpit—all made of mud. Asked then why he hadn't made a preacher, the boy smiled and said, "I hain't got *mud* enough."

Nicolay told his fiancée, "Going into his room this morning to announce the Secretary of War I found a little party of Quakers holding a prayer meeting around him, and he was compelled to bear the affliction until the 'spirit' moved them to stop. Isn't it strange that so many and such intelligent people often have so little common sense?"[19]

"The Best Gift God Has Given to Man"

Chapter 7

There undoubtedly was an influence of the churches and of the clergy upon Lincoln as President, but it cannot have been a dominant one in the development of his faith. He was strengthened in realizing that most Northern church opinion supported his steps toward emancipation. The churches were valued as interpreters of God's plan for the nation. He was grateful for their humanitarian work and their pastoral concern for the wounded and the bereaved. Yet the rock on which he stood was the Bible. Here he found help in interpreting the nation's history in the light of its great motifs of judgment, punishment, justice, mercy, and reconciliation. No President has ever had the detailed knowledge of the Bible that Lincoln had. No President has ever woven its thought and its rhythms into the warp and woof of his state papers as he did.

The "First Lecture on Discoveries and Inventions" which he delivered in 1858 before the Young Men's Association of Bloomington is chiefly an exegesis of the Bible, particularly of Genesis, to show the origin of clothing, weaving, toolmaking, and transportation. He must have written this with Cruden's Concordance open on his desk, for there are at least thirty-four references to the Bible in this manuscript in his own hand. The type of argument employed by his Springfield pastor, Dr. James Smith, in *The Christian's Defense* is used by Lincoln to reconcile newer scientific findings with biblical chronology. "The . . . mention of *'thread'* by Abraham is the oldest recorded allusion to spinning and weaving; and *it* was made about two thousand years after the creation of man, and now, near four thousand years ago. Profane authors think these arts originated in Egypt; and this is not contradicted, or made improbable, by anything in the Bible; for the allusion of Abraham, mentioned, was not made until after he had sojourned in Egypt."[1]

Lincoln's knowledge of the Bible was so thorough that his political opponents generally found themselves on dangerous ground when they quoted it against him. When Judge Douglas somewhat fantastically cited Adam and Eve as the first beneficiaries of his doctrine of "popular sovereignty" Lincoln corrected him. "God did not place good and evil before man, telling him to make his choice. On the contrary, he did tell him there was one tree, of the fruit of which he should not eat, upon pain of certain death." Then added Lincoln pointedly, "I should scarcely wish so strong a prohibition against slavery in Nebraska."[2]

News was brought to Lincoln that the dissident Republicans

had nominated Fremont at their Cleveland convention in May 1864. When told that instead of the thousands that had been advertised as participants only four hundred had actually come, he immediately found the number significant. Reaching for his Bible, he turned quickly to I Samuel 22:2 and read about David in the Cave of Adullam: "And every one that was in distress, and every one that was in debt, and every one that was discontented, gathered themselves unto him; and he became a captain over them: and there were with him about four hundred men."[3]

So much a part of him was the world of the Bible with its stories and characters that much of his humor flowed between its familiar banks. A typical story is the incident related by Senator Henderson of Missouri, who called on Lincoln some months before the emancipation of the slaves. Lincoln complained of being hounded by the abolitionists spearheaded by Charles Sumner, Henry Wilson, and Thaddeus Stevens. Just then as Lincoln looked out of the window he saw the three determined congressmen crossing the White House lawn to his door. His sad face lit up and a sparkle came into his eyes.

"Henderson, did you ever attend an old blab school? Yes? Well, so did I, and what little schooling I got in early life was in that way. I attended such a school in a log schoolhouse in Indiana where we had no reading books or grammars, and all our reading was done from the Bible. We stood in a long line and read in turn from it. One day our lesson was the story of the three Hebrew children and their escape from the fiery furnace. It fell to a little towheaded fellow who stood next to me to read for the first time the verse with the unpronounceable names.

He made a sorry mess of Shadrach and Meshach, and went all to pieces on Abednego. Whereupon the master boxed his ears until he sobbed aloud. Then the lesson went on, each boy in the class reading a verse in turn. Finally the towheaded boy stopped crying, but only to fix his gaze upon the verses ahead, and set up a yell of surprise and alarm. The master demanded the reason for this unexpected outbreak. 'Look there, master,' said the boy, pointing his finger at the verse which in a few moments he would be expected to read, and at the three proper names which it contained, 'there comes them same damn three fellows again!' "[4]

Lincoln enjoyed quoting a text as his immediate response to something said to him. He deflated the somewhat pompous Lord Lyons, the British ambassador, who made an official call to announce formally to the President in the name of his gracious sovereign Queen Victoria the betrothal of the Prince of Wales to the Princess Alexandra of Denmark. Said Lincoln to the bachelor ambassador when he had finished his communication, "Go thou and do likewise."

Next to this type of repartee, he liked to quote Scripture in answer to Scripture. Hugh McCulloch, an official of the Treasury Department, once introduced a delegation of New York bankers with much deference. Speaking of their patriotism and loyalty in holding the securities of the nation, he clinched his commendation of them with the text: "Where the treasure is there will the heart be also." Lincoln, like a crack of the whip, rejoined, "There is another text, Mr. McCulloch, which might apply, 'Where the carcass is, there will the eagles be gathered together.' "[5]

It would be possible to multiply illustrations of his sharpness in tracking down biblical texts. More significant than these items for his maturing faith is his view of the authority of the Bible as revelation for him. His words to Speed—to the effect that Speed should take all of the Bible that he could on reason and the rest on faith and he would live and die a happier man—have already been recorded. Lincoln spelled out this conviction with even greater clarity in his response on September 7, 1864, to the loyal colored people of Baltimore, who presented him with a magnificently bound Bible as a token of their appreciation of his work for the Negro. This is one of the great documents of Lincoln's religious confession. His reference to the Savior's communication of good to the world, his conviction that the knowledge of right and wrong springs from revelation, and his belief that human destiny is illuminated by its teachings need more emphasis than they have generally had in studies of his religion.

"In regard to this Great Book, I have but to say, it is the best gift God has given to man. All the good the Savior gave to the world was communicated through this book. But for it we could not know right from wrong. All things most desirable for man's welfare, here and hereafter, are to be found portrayed in it."[6]

This public statement of belief in the Bible was carried further in a conversation which L. E. Chittenden, the register of the Treasury, recorded in his *Recollections*.

"The character of the Bible," said Lincoln, "is easily established, at least to my satisfaction. We have to believe many things that we do not comprehend. The Bible is the only one that claims to be God's Book—to comprise his law—his history. It contains an immense amount of evidence of its own authenticity. It describes a Governor omnipotent enough to operate this great machine, and declares that He made it. It states other facts which we do not fully comprehend, but which we cannot account for. What shall we do with them?

"Now," continued Lincoln, "let us treat the Bible fairly. If we had a witness on the stand whose general story we knew was true, we would believe him when he asserted facts of which we had no other evidence. We ought to treat the Bible with equal fairness. I decided a long time ago that it was less difficult to believe that the Bible was what it claimed to be than to disbelieve it. It is a good book for us to obey—it contains the Ten Commandments, the Golden Rule, and many other rules which ought to be followed. No man was ever the worse for living according to the directions of the Bible."[7]

The Second Inaugural Address was to be the climactic expression of this biblical faith. It reads like a supplement to the Bible. In it there are fourteen references to God, four direct quotations from Genesis, Psalms, and Matthew, and other allusions to scriptural teaching. The London *Spectator* commented prophetically on this Scripture-steeped masterpiece: "We cannot read it without a renewed conviction that it is the noblest political document known to history, and should have for the nation and the statesmen he left behind him something of a sacred and almost prophetic character. Surely, none was ever written under a stronger sense of the reality of God's government. And certainly none written in a period of passionate conflict ever so completely excluded the partiality of victorious faction, and breathed so pure a strain of mingled justice and mercy."[8]

Sandburg shows an artist's appreciation of unity when he brackets Lincoln's laughter and his religion in a one-chapter discussion in Volume III of *The War Years*. They belong together. Humor is the threshold to the religious despite a widespread belief derived from a dour Puritanism that they are poles apart. Philosophically they are close, but they diverge at a critical point. In his *Concluding Unscientific Postscript* the Danish thinker Soren Kierkegaard describes humor as a boundary zone between an ethical evaluation of life and a religious one.

In humor a man is beginning to sit loose to his own anxious hold on life. There are, of course, stages in this development. Some people can laugh at others but not at the foibles and pretensions of the self. Such laughter is usually ironic and isolating. Others can laugh at themselves. This is real humor, free of bitter irony, that binds men in a community of appreciation. While Lincoln on occasion did employ irony and sarcasm, his basic humor was one that sat so loose to the claims of the self that it deflated those at odds with him. This is exactly why, besides just enjoying laughter for its own sake, Lincoln told stories. They saved time, enabling him to make his point unmistakably clear without subjecting his listeners to any self-righteousness of his own in the position he wished to maintain. Like parables, they shift responsibility from the narrator to his hearers.

In 1863, according to Colonel Silas W. Burt, a military delegation waited on Lincoln. When they prepared to leave, one who had had too much to drink slapped the President on the leg and asked for one of his "good" stories. Turning to the embarrassed group, Lincoln said, "I believe I have the popular reputation of being a storyteller, but I do not deserve the name in its general sense, for it is not the story itself, but its purpose or effect that interests me. I often avoid a long and useless discussion by others, or a laborious explanation on my own part, by a short story that illustrates my point of view. So too, the sharpness of a refusal or the edge of a rebuke may be blunted by an appropriate story so as to save wounded feelings and yet serve the purpose. No, I am not simply a storyteller, but storytelling as an emollient saves me friction and distress."[9]

Herndon, who was constitutionally incapable of appreciating Lincoln's religion, was just as obtuse on his humor. After a long-winded disquisition the partner concluded in a psychosomatic diagnosis that Lincoln told jokes because they served as a "stimulant, sending more blood to the brain, [which] aroused the whole man to an active consciousness— sense of his surroundings."[10]

An excellent illustration of how Lincoln employed humor to cool down opposition comes from an encounter with Senator Fessenden of Maine. The story also shows his ability as a humorist in exploiting the incongruities of life. He deflates his angry friend by linking types of profanity with types of denominational confession. Fessenden, enraged over an issue of patronage, exploded to Lincoln, losing control of himself in abusive profanity. Lincoln waited until his rage was spent and then asked softly, "You are an Episcopalian, aren't you,

Senator?" "Yes, sir," said his opponent stiffly, "I belong to that church." "I thought so," said Lincoln. "You Episcopalians all swear alike. Seward is an Episcopalian. But Stanton is a Presbyterian. You ought to hear him swear." He then analyzed blasphemy into its major theological variants. A somewhat chastened and sheepish Fessenden sat down then to talk quietly about patronage.[11]

The story illustrates the non-pharisaic perspective of Lincoln and provides the point of transition from humor to religion. Humor partially frees us from our anxious clutching at existence by providing an outlook independent, to a degree, of the self. Religion deepens the perspective by making the self see that God is in control of the world, thereby reducing the self-assertion of the ego. Humor deals with the proximate incongruities of existence, religion with the ultimate incongruities. Reinhold Niebuhr puts the relationship in a graphic image: ". . . there is laughter in the vestibule of the temple, the echo of laughter in the temple itself, but only faith and prayer, and no laughter, in the holy of holies."[12]

One of the greatnesses of Lincoln was the way he held to strong moral positions without the usual accompaniment of self-righteousness or smugness. He expressed this rare achievement provisionally in his humor and in an ultimate dimension in his religious evaluations. To the Pennsylvania delegation that congratulated him after the inauguration he said, urging forbearance and respect for differences of opinion between the states, "I would inculcate this idea, so that we may not, like Pharisees, set ourselves up to be better than other people."[13]

The Puritan in religion has found it difficult to submit himself in his moral rectitude to higher judgment when he judges his fellows. This accounts for much of the pride and lovelessness of organized Christianity. Lincoln expressed the antipharisaic side of the Christian gospel more poignantly and winsomely than most ecclesiastics. For him humor was closely related to his religious perspective. He is said to have enjoyed and even encouraged the spreading of a newspaper story about him. Two Quaker women were overheard on a train in the following dialogue:

"I think Jefferson will succeed."

"Why does thee think so?"

"Because Jefferson is a praying man."

"And so is Abraham a praying man."

"Yes, but the Lord will think Abraham is joking."

This story perfectly illustrates the relationship of humor and faith in Lincoln. The fact that Lincoln also appreciated it tends to show that he too was aware of their closeness in his make-up. Sandburg after recording this incident speculates as to whether there was here in germinal form that dilemma wherein "both read the same Bible and pray to the same God; and each invokes his aid against the other."

The picture then of Lincoln in the White House as the man of prayer needs the supplement of Lincoln the man of laughter. This was the Lincoln who served as a nucleus for many joke books, the Lincoln with a fund of anecdotes and especially a plentiful supply of preacher stories, the Lincoln who roared at the writings of Artemus Ward and kept the comic narratives about the Rev. Petroleum V. Nasby in his desk with his state papers. Once when he had been reading a selection from Ward to the Cabinet he looked up to see a circle of unsmiling and uncomprehending faces. "Gentlemen," he said, "why don't you laugh? If I didn't laugh under the strain that is upon me day and night, I should go mad. And you need that medicine as well as I."

There was development in his humor as in his faith. His first stories were told chiefly to amuse and divert his audience. Gradually his stories took on more purposiveness and served as vehicles to communicate his point of view quickly and effectively. Two examples will be given, the first from his New Salem period and the second from the presidency.

In New Salem Lincoln described an old-line Baptist preacher who chose as his text: "I am the Christ whom I shall represent today." His shirt and pants of coarse linen were anchored with one button at the waist and another at the neck. As he waxed eloquent, a blue lizard worked its way up his leg. Slapping did no good. Finally a desperate wrench and a kick resulted in nothing less than the loss of his pants. Repeating his text, the preacher valiantly struggled on, but now the lizard was tickling his back. A second convulsion fixed the lizard, but also resulted in the loss of the tow shirt. The congregation sat in silent horror. Then an old lady arose and addressed herself to the unclad preacher: If you represent Christ, then I'm done with the Bible."[14]

A prominent Presbyterian preacher of Southern sympathies, the Rev. Dr. McPheeters, found that he had been locked out of his St. Louis church by the commanding general of the area. Both factions in the congregation sent representatives to the President, who listened attentively to their conflicting statements and positions. It reminded Lincoln of an Illinois farmer and his son John who were hunting down a hog that had repeatedly ravaged their melon patch. The trail led up a muddy creek with the hog continually crossing the stream to the exhaustion and impatience of the hunters. "John," said the father, "you cross over and go up on that side, and I'll keep on this side, for I believe the old fellow is on both sides." "Gentlemen," said Lincoln to his quarrelsome delegation, "that is just where I stand in regard to your controversies in St. Louis. I am on both sides. I can't allow my generals to run the churches, and I can't allow you ministers to preach rebellion. Go home, preach the gospel, stand by the Union, and don't disturb the Government any more."[15]

Both the humor and the faith endeared Lincoln to the people. Both were complementary aspects of his nature. "Two strains," said Benjamin Thomas in a skillful study of his humor, "—pioneer exaggeration and Yankee laconicism—met in him. In his humor, as in his rise from obscurity to fame and in his simple, democratic faith and thought, he epitomized the American ideal."[16]

Chapter 8

In Lincoln's wrestling with the responsibilities of the presidency his religious evaluation of his own role and of the nation's history became more clearly defined and then conjoined. A deepened personal faith led to a surer grasp of the rootage of American democracy in the will of God. Lincoln was aware of a process of development going on within himself, for he told his friend Noah Brooks that "he did not remember any precise time when he passed through any special change of purpose, or of heart; but he would say that his own election to office, and the crisis immediately following, influentially determined him in what he called 'a process of crystallization,' then going on in his mind."[1]

Here is the explanation for the many speeches and comments on that long train trip from Springfield to Washington which some historians of politics have found so barren. They criticize him for a lack of policy during this period. His own Secretary of State within a month after the beginning of his administration complained of the same problem. The truth of the matter is that Lincoln was never a person with a doctrinaire program ready for all possible events. There was a strong element of pragmatism in his make-up that was actually one of his greatest strengths. This pragmatism was rooted not primarily in political opportunism, or in a weak vacillation of decision, but in an inner resolution to obey the will of God. Because he believed deeply that God guided history he sought humbly and patiently to learn his assignment in the drama. His faith freed him from the illusion of titanism and from the frantic stance of an Atlas bearing the burden of the world alone upon his bruised shoulders.

What he said again and again on that trip to the nation's capital was that reliance on the divine will was the nation's real strength and that the American people and the President were instruments in the hands of the God of history. This was the background for his emphasis upon national renewal and national regeneration. These themes have been analyzed in the First Inaugural and in the Fast Day Proclamation after the disaster at Bull Run. They were pithily condensed into the concluding line of his message to the special session of Congress in July 1861: ". . . let us renew our trust in God and go forward without fear, and with manly hearts."[2] They would rise again to sublime expression two years later at Gettysburg.

There is testimony to the effect that Lincoln found the book of Job a source of strength in the White House. That ancient patriarch, stripped of possessions, family, and health, dared in dialogue to challenge the Almighty. Out of the whirlwind God replied that the mystery of suffering was too great for one as finite as Job to grasp, but if he could not understand the divine answer he was at least blessed in his resolute faith, which had retained its fidelity and integrity when all outward supports had been smashed.

Undoubtedly Lincoln resembled Job in being a wrestler with God. The match, however, was of a different order. Lincoln never questioned the ultimate justice of God. That was a settled conviction that gave his struggle a different twist than Job's. Lincoln's battle was to read "the signs of the times," to learn what the will of God actually demanded in the conflicting events of his day. Lincoln did not question the supremacy of the God before Whom "the nations are as the small dust of the balance." He questioned how to know that divine will in the day-to-day responsibilities of a nation at war with itself. He sought to avoid both the futility and the rebellion of opposing God's purposes in history. He would not use his ax vainly to split across the grain. The problem was to know the direction of the grain when so many honest men disagreed.

He told his callers many times that his concern was not to get God on his side, but to be quite sure that he and the nation were on God's side. An interview in June 1862 with a delegation from Iowa led by Congressman James Wilson threw more light on this point. It revealed again Lincoln's strong predestinarian conviction about God's will. A member was pressing Lincoln for more resolute action on emancipation, saying, "Slavery must be stricken down wherever it exists. If we do not do right I believe God will let us go our own way to our ruin. But if we do right, I believe He will lead us safely out of this wilderness, crown our arms with victory, and restore our now dissevered Union."

With a sparkle in his eyes and with his right arm outstretched toward the speaker, Lincoln agreed about the judgments of the God of history but added with great emphasis: "My faith is greater than yours. . . . I also believe He will compel us to do right in order that He may do these things, not so much because we desire them as that they accord with His plans of dealing with this nation, in the midst of which He means to establish justice. I think He means that we shall do more than we have yet done in furtherance of His plans, and He will open the way for our doing it. I have felt His hand upon me in great trials and submitted to His guidance, and I trust that as He shall further open the way I will be ready to walk therein, relying on His help and trusting in His goodness and wisdom." Wilson recorded that his manner of delivery was most impressive. Lincoln continued, saying that military reverses were to be expected. "Sometimes it seems necessary that we should be confronted with perils which threaten us with disaster in order that we may not get puffed up and forget Him who has much work for us yet to do."[3]

In the documents of 1861 Lincoln had urged the nation to see the hand of God in the outbreak of the war and in the Union reverses. His concern beyond that period was to understand more concretely the will of God in respect to the causation and continuance of the bloody conflict. The mounting lists of the dead and the wounded drove him in anguish to ultimate answers about the purpose of the war. He began to find these in terms of the providence of God in respect to slavery and the future of democratic government in all the earth. Among his papers after his death was discovered an undated document which he had not intended, said Nicolay and Hay, "to be seen of men." It was a meditation on the prevailing of God's will. It brought the themes already discussed—predestination, human instrumentalities, and God's effectual direction of men's actions—into burning focus around God's purpose for the nation. His secretaries gave a late September 1862 date to the autograph, but the Rutgers editors have chosen an early one in September. This would associate the document with Lincoln's despair following the second battle of Bull Run when Attorney General Bates reported that he "seemed wrung by the bitterest anguish." This date would also provide a point of transition to his decision in late September that he must free the slaves to save the Union. The meditation reveals theological profundity and legal precision of definition.

"The will of God prevails. In great contests each party claims to act in accordance with the will of God. Both *may* be, and one *must* be wrong. God cannot be *for*, and *against* the same thing at the same time. In the present civil war it is quite possible that God's purpose is something different from the purpose of either party—and yet the human instrumentalities, working just as they do, are of the best adaptation to effect His purpose. I am almost ready to say this is probably true—that God wills this contest, and wills that it shall not end yet. By His mere quiet power, on the minds of the now contestants, He could have either *saved* or *destroyed* the Union without a human contest. Yet the contest began. And, having begun, He could give the final victory to either side any day. Yet the contest proceeds."[4]

By September 22, 1862, Lincoln had determined to issue a preliminary proclamation of emancipation. He had, as was discussed in Chapter I, "made a solemn vow before God" to act for the slaves as soon as a Union victory should give stature to his action, following on this point the earlier advice of Seward. Antietam had been won in the previous week and Lee's army had withdrawn across the Potomac into Virginia. The making of this vow was by no means the irresponsible resort to superstition that it has seemed to some. The method obviously had dangers if it were lightly undertaken as a flipping of a coin for a divine decision, but such an irresponsible procedure was not Lincoln's. His action was preceded by the blood, sweat, and tears of a struggle to know the will of God on the Union and on slavery amid the problems of his constitutional powers and oath and the effect of such contemplated action on the North, on the border states, on the South, and finally on the world. The historian Randall comments perceptively on Lincoln's decision: "If these deliberations had given him humility, and a sense of association with Divine Purpose (which was more than once indicated), they had also given executive confidence. In reaching his important decision there is ample reason to believe that Lincoln had not only endured anxious hours, but had undergone a significant inner experience from which he emerged with quiet serenity."[5]

The solemn vow and covenant may have been more in

conformance with Old Testament than with New Testament religion, but the practice was imbedded in Lincoln's biblical piety and came to him as part of the religious heritage of the nation.

Behind Lincoln's act in establishing covenant with the God of nations on the issue of emancipation lay the conviction that America was a chosen nation destined to further God's plan for mankind. This faith, rooted in the development of New England theology, must be studied in some detail if we are rightly to understand Lincoln's convictions. In an essay entitled "The Union as Religious Mysticism" Edmund Wilson claims that "Lincoln's conception of the progress and meaning of the Civil War was indeed an interpretation that he partly took over from others but that he partly made others accept. . . . Like most of the important products of the American mind at that time, it grew out of the religious tradition of the New England theology of Puritanism."[6]

The American dream was the later flowering of the Puritan conception of New England as God's new land of promise and of the colonization of these rocky shores as the new exodus over the Red Sea and Jordan, bringing religious liberty to God's elect. The kernel was already present in the text from which John Cotton preached to the emigration under Governor Winthrop. "Moreover I will appoint a place for my people Israel, and will plant them, that they may dwell in a place of their own, and move no more; neither shall the children of wickedness afflict them any more . . ."[7]

Combining these special interpretations with the rigor of Calvin's doctrine of predestination, the New England divines believed fervently in the religious destiny of their commonwealth. It became important to keep open the channels through which God could make known His will to His people in the day-to-day events that were occurring. King Philip's savage Indian war was minutely studied to understand why God was punishing His people in its disasters while its deliverances were gratefully recorded as "particular providences."

The outlook on life furthered by this sense of mission and destiny, while it might have doctrinaire concepts, was actually the very opposite of a closed or static system. Each new configuration of revelatory events required a fresh openness for man to understand God's current visitation. Hence an attitude of pragmatism sprang up, with the result that developing forms of democratic government became increasingly responsive to this fact. In the complicated currents of the eighteenth century a humanitarian rationalism began to erode the explicitly religious upland of the previous century. It did not, however, change the forward-looking orientation or the pragmatic spirit. Indeed it reinforced it with perfectionist impulses of its own. This interesting evolution can be charted in two dimensions: (1) the function of the people in a democracy and (2) the democratic means to further this function.

In the Puritan interpretation the people became aware that they were instruments of Providence. This was slowly transmuted into a reliance upon the people as the corporate bearer of God's wisdom. The people's wisdom would be expressed in the long run by means of majority rule. Here is the original root for the adage that the will of the people is the will of God. We have had numerous examples of Lincoln's confidence in the essential rightness and wisdom of the people. This explains his belief, expressed at Buffalo, that God's will is ultimately to be known *through* the people. "I must trust in that Supreme Being who has never forsaken this favored land, through the instrumentality of this great and intelligent people."

He had expressed this belief as early as 1850 in his eulogy at the death of President Taylor. "Yet, under all circumstances, trusting to our Maker, and through His wisdom and beneficence, to the great body of our people, we will not despair, nor despond."[8]

This is also the philosophy behind the well-known remark attributed to him about fooling the people. Governor Fifer of Illinois claimed he had heard Milton Hay quote Lincoln: "You can fool some of the people all of the time and all of the people some of the time, but you can't fool all of the people all of the time." It is behind his statement that "we cannot escape history." In the long run there is no appeal from history to any higher court for the simple reason that history has been woven on God's loom.

The Puritan conception of the people's task required in addition that the will of God could only be known provided all channels of communication were kept open. The resolution not to allow the Spirit to be fenced in was gradually expressed in governmental structure by granting to religious groups freedom from state control. This freedom was in turn transmuted into the obligation so eloquently stated by Jefferson that a majority must not suppress its minorities. Only in such a free atmosphere could truth itself be furthered by the clash of opinion. The eighteenth century expressed the older concept of openness to the Spirit's direction in terms of the essential equality of all men in possessing certain inalienable rights. These were, of course, spelled out in the Bill of Rights as amendments to the Constitution.

Lincoln's passages in the First Inaugural about majority rule illustrated perfectly the point that the wisdom of the people could be expressed only through majority rule that preserved openness for minority groups. "A majority held in restraint by constitutional checks, and limitations, and always changing easily with deliberate changes of popular opinions and sentiments, is the only true sovereign of a free people. Whoever rejects it does, of necessity, fly to anarchy or to despotism. . . . Why should there not be a patient confidence in the ultimate justice of the people? Is there any better or equal hope in the world?"[9]

One of the means for holding a majority to responsibility was the system of checks and balances in the Constitution to keep power dispersed as much as possible. The doctrine of man behind this is, of course, not the view of his essential goodness which has sometimes been offered as the rationale for democracy, but a realistic view of the selfishness in human nature. Lincoln argued that human nature as such could not be changed. "The Bible says somewhere that we are desperately selfish. I think we would have discovered that fact without the Bible."[10] In other words, man is good enough to make democracy possible and bad enough to make it necessary.

The Puritan heritage distilled through the eighteenth-century patriots without, however, loss of its original religious strength explains many features in Lincoln's thought. It is the background for the predestinating will of God, for corporate and individual responsibility, for the direction of democracy as a way, for America as "God's almost chosen people," for belief in the wisdom of the people, for the possibility of making a solemn vow and covenant with God and observing its historical results, for the importance of "discerning the signs of the times," and even for the Gettysburg note, not of victory, but of "testing" the nation's vocation. In subsequent speeches and letters he would articulate, deepen, and reattest this heritage until he became in Sidney Mead's perceptive phrase "the spiritual center of American history."[11]

About a month after issuing the preliminary proclamation of emancipation Lincoln had an interesting interview with a distinguished Quaker lady. Mrs. Eliza Gurney was the widow of Joseph Gurney, the English Friend, writer, and philanthropist. She came to the White House and talked with the President about seeking divine guidance. Lincoln had great sympathy for the dilemma of the Friends. Pacifist on the one hand, they hated war. Strongly anti-slavery on the other, they saw that only on the anvil of war could emancipation be actually forged. Lincoln had a way of transcending the clash of religious absolutes while not withdrawing from responsible and resolute action. He would explain this dilemma in his Second Inaugural.

After Mrs. Gurney knelt and "uttered a short but most beautiful, eloquent and comprehensive prayer that light and wisdom might be shed down from on high, to guide our President," Lincoln gave the answer that has been preserved in the Lincoln papers:

"I am glad of this interview, and glad to know that I have your sympathy and prayers. We are indeed going through a great trial—a fiery trial. In the very responsible position in which I happen to be placed, being a humble instrument in the hands of our Heavenly Father, as I am, and as we all are, to work out His great purposes, I have desired that all my works and acts may be according to His will, and that it might be so, I have sought His aid—but if after endeavoring to do my best in the light which He affords me, I find my efforts fail, I must believe that for some purpose unknown to me, He wills it otherwise. If I had had my way, this war would never have been commenced; if I had been allowed my way this war would have been ended before this, but we find it still continues; and we must believe that He permits it for some wise purpose of His own, mysterious and unknown to us; and though with our limited understandings we may not be able to comprehend it, yet we cannot but believe, that He who made the world still governs it."[12]

There is an interesting sequel to this dialogue. One year later Mrs. Gurney sent a letter to the President by the hand of a mutual friend, Isaac Newton. She wrote "to give thee the assurance of my continued hearty sympathy in all thy heavy burthens and responsibilities and to express, not only my own earnest prayer, but I believe the prayer of many thousands whose hearts thou hast gladdened by the praiseworthy and *successful* effort to 'burst the bands of wickedness, and let the oppressed go free' that the Almighty . . . may strengthen thee to accomplish *all* the blessed purposes, which, in the unerring counsel of his will and wisdom, I do assuredly believe he did design to make thee instrumental in accomplishing, when he appointed thee thy present post of vast responsibility as the Chief Magistrate. . . ."

Lincoln wrote an answer that shows his deep respect for his correspondent and breathes an air of religious confidence at the very time that Union hopes had been dashed by Early's raid to the outskirts of Washington, the failure of Burnside at the Petersburg crater, and widespread Copperhead disturbances in the North.

"My esteemed friend. I have not forgotten—probably never shall forget—the very impressive occasion when yourself and friends visited me on a Sabbath forenoon two years ago. Nor has your kind letter, written, nearly a year later, ever been forgotten. In all, it has been your purpose to strengthen my reliance on God. I am much indebted to the good Christian people of the country for their constant prayers and consolations; and to no one of them, more than to yourself. The purposes of the Almighty are perfect, and must prevail, though we erring mortals may fail to accurately perceive them in advance. We hoped for a happy termination of this terrible war long before this; but God knows best, and has ruled otherwise. We shall yet acknowledge His wisdom and our own error therein. Meanwhile we must work earnestly in the best light He gives us, trusting that so working still conduces to the great ends He ordains. Surely He intends some great good to follow this mighty convulsion, which no mortal could make, and no mortal could stay.

"Your people—the Friends—have had, and are having, a very great trial. On principle, and faith, opposed to both war and oppression, they can only practically oppose oppression by war. In this hard dilemma, some have chosen one horn and some the other. For those appealing to me on conscientious grounds, I have done, and shall do, the best I could and can, in my own conscience, under my oath to the law. That you believe this I doubt not; and believing it, I shall still receive, for our country and myself, your earnest prayers to our Father in Heaven. Your sincere friend—A. Lincoln."[13]

In a talk once with his register of the Treasury, L. E. Chittenden, Lincoln spelled out further his sense of being directed by God's will. His reported words have a concreteness about them that marks a considerable advance beyond the view of his 1846 handbill, but the structure of analysis is continuous with it.

"That the Almighty does make use of human agencies, and directly intervenes in human affairs, is one of the plainest statements in the Bible. I have had so many evidences of His direction, so many instances when I have been controlled by some other power than my own will, that I cannot doubt that this power comes from above. I frequently see my way clear to a decision when I am conscious that I have no sufficient facts upon which to found it. But I cannot recall one instance in which I have followed my own judgment, founded upon such a decision, when the results were unsatisfactory; whereas, in almost every instance when I have yielded to the views of others, I have had occasion to regret it. I am satisfied that, when the Almighty wants me to do or not to do, a particular thing, he finds a way of letting me know it."[14]

Lincoln's concern at this period to be open to the divine will found expression about a month after the preliminary proclamation of emancipation was issued. It took the form of an order for Sabbath observance in the armed forces and listed among the supporting reasons "a due regard for the Divine will." Lincoln turned to General Washington for precedent. "The first General Order issued by the Father of his country after the Declaration of Independence, indicates the spirit in which our institutions were founded and should ever be defended. 'The General hopes and trusts that every officer and man will endeavor to live and act as becomes a Christian soldier defending the dearest rights and liberties of his country.' "[15]

The high peak, however, in Lincoln's desire to obey the divine will was revealed in his annual message to Congress on December 1, 1862. Here his imagination soared as he pictured the special destiny of America freed of slavery as a means to the advance of freedom and democracy over all the earth. He suggested three constitutional amendments for the gradual and compensated emancipation of slaves owned by loyal masters and for voluntary colonization abroad for freedmen. The theme of slavery began to yield to the larger theme of democracy "as the last, best hope of earth." This association had been made before by Lincoln, but henceforth it appears with more persuasiveness and conviction as one of God's purposes being forged in the fires of civil conflict. The religious impulse was the same for the drive to eliminate slavery as it was for the realization of a brave new world. It was the conviction of the declaration that all men are created equal regarded progressively as the expression of God's will for "the great family of man." It meant every human son of man under whatever type of government. This vision was based not on humanistic utopianism but on an apocalyptic revelation of God's purpose for mankind.

This speech is supported by such artistry of words that it remains the masterpiece of Lincoln's longer speeches. Its opening paragraph provides the theological framework and points toward the great peroration at the end. God's guidance is sought for responsible action.

"Since your last annual assembling another year of health and bountiful harvests has passed. And while it has not pleased the Almighty to bless us with a return of peace, we can but press on, guided by the best light He gives us, trusting that in His own good time, and wise way, all will yet be well."

The sureness of his touch can be seen as he uses a biblical quotation to underscore his point on the physical inseparability of the United States.

"A nation may be said to consist of its territory, its people, and its laws. The territory is the only part which is of certain durability. 'One generation passeth away, and another generation cometh, but the earth abideth forever.' It is of the first importance to duly consider, and estimate, this ever-enduring part."

After pleading for a fresh approach to action on the slavery issue he begins the great concluding paragraph with its oft-quoted phrase, "we cannot escape history." Lincoln might have said, "we cannot escape God," for what he means is that history is controlled and determined by God and that it is futile for man to oppose its plan. Lincoln speaks as a prophet disclosing the oracle of God for the Union and for the world.

"Fellow citizens, *we* cannot escape history. . . . The fiery trial through which we pass, will light us down, in honor or dishonor, to the latest generation. We *say* we are for the Union. The world will not forget that we say this. We know how to save the Union. The world knows we do know how to save it. We—even *we here*—hold the power, and bear the responsibility. In *giving* freedom to the *slave,* we *assure* freedom to the *free*—honorable alike in what we give, and what we preserve. We shall nobly save, or meanly lose, the last, best hope of earth. Other means may succeed; this could not fail. The way is plain, peaceful, generous, just—a way which, if followed, the world will forever applaud, and God must forever bless."[16]

On January 1, 1863, Lincoln issued the Final Proclamation of Emancipation, freeing forever the slaves within the areas then in rebellion against the United States. He gratefully accepted Secretary Chase's suggestion of the words "a solemn recognition of responsibility before men and before God" in the document. He incorporated Chase's wording verbatim except for clarifying his view that the action was constitutional as a war measure. "And upon this act, sincerely believed to be an act of justice, warranted by the Constitution, upon military necessity, I invoke the considerate judgment of mankind and the gracious favor of Almighty God."[17]

Chapter 9

The year 1863 began with great military anxieties. At Murfreesboro, Tennessee, Confederate General Bragg smashed the right
wing of Rosecrans's Army of the Cumberland. After days of
savage fighting and heavy casualties General George Thomas
stabilized the situation for the North as the Confederates with-
drew toward Chattanooga. In the East with the Army of the
Potomac the immediate but enduring crisis was one of command. Burnside's earlier defeat at Fredericksburg had cost him
the confidence of his subordinates. Finally Lincoln had to dis-
miss him, taking in his stead Joseph Hooker. The President
reprimanded Hooker in the famous letter for his disloyalty to
Burnside and for his foolish clamoring for a dictator.

The immediate impact of emancipation was disappointing.
Since it was unaccompanied by Union victories it was ineffectual

in the only areas in which it was authoritative. Democrats accused the President of tricking them into supporting a war for the Union in order to convert it into a crusade against slavery. When Lincoln came to see that plans for sending the Negroes to other areas as colonists could not be implemented, he began to use them as soldiers in order to help the Union and to give them increased stature among their white neighbors.

Slowly expressions of support for emancipation began to trickle in from England, France, and other countries. The workingmen of Manchester, England, had been thrown into dire want and widespread unemployment by the blockade on Southern cotton. Yet they supported Lincoln's stand. The President expressed his gratitude for their resolutions "as an instance of sublime Christian heroism which has not been surpassed in any age or in any country."[1]

At the suggestion of Senator Harlan of Iowa, Congress passed a resolution calling upon the President to set apart a day for national prayer and humiliation. The text of this Senate document was somewhat remarkable for its explicitly Christian reference to seeking "Him for succour according to His appointed way, through Jesus Christ." "Fully concurring in the views of the Senate," Lincoln named April 30, 1863, as a National Fast Day. He counseled personal and national repentance. The Bible and the course of history, he argued, showed the necessity for a nation to acknowledge God.

". . . it is the duty of nations as well as of men, to own their dependence upon the overruling power of God, to confess their sins and transgressions, in humble sorrow, yet with assured hope that genuine repentance will lead to mercy and pardon;

and to recognize the sublime truth, announced in the Holy Scriptures and proven by all history, that those nations only are blessed whose God is the Lord."[2]

He then passed beyond the terms of his proclamation after Bull Run by assigning definite reasons for this punishment of war. The entire nation and not just the South was guilty of presumptuous sins which had to be corrected. The document resembled a page from Amos, or Isaiah, or Jeremiah.

"And, insomuch as we know that, by His divine law, nations like individuals are subjected to punishments and chastisements in this world, may we not justly fear that the awful calamity of civil war, which now desolates the land, may be but a punishment, inflicted upon us, for our presumptuous sins, to the needful end of our national reformation as a whole People?"

Unwilling to allow even this statement of sin to remain in the abstract, Lincoln confronted the nation with forgetfulness of God, pride, foolish imagination, and the illusion of Lordship. It was as though he had paraphrased Luther's statement that the essence of sin is the sinner's unwillingness to admit that he is a sinner, when he charged the nation with forgetting its need for redemption.

"We have been the recipients of the choicest bounties of Heaven. We have been preserved, these many years, in peace and prosperity. We have grown in numbers, wealth and power, as no other nation has ever grown. But we have forgotten God. We have forgotten the gracious hand which preserved us in peace, and multiplied and enriched and strengthened us; and we have vainly imagined, in the deceitfulness of our hearts, that all these blessings were produced by some superior wisdom and virtue of our own. Intoxicated with unbroken success, we have become too self-sufficient to feel the necessity of redeeming and preserving grace, too proud to pray to the God that made us!"

Lincoln then named the date for the national fast and urged the people to keep "the day holy to the Lord" by appropriate exercises in church and in home. He closed with the assurance that God would accept and bless a repentant people.

"All this being done, in sincerity and truth, let us then rest humbly in the hope authorized by the Divine teachings, that the united cry of the Nation will be heard on high, and answered with blessings, no less than the pardon of our national sins, and the restoration of our now divided and suffering Country, to its former happy condition of unity and peace."

Within a month of the issuance of this Proclamation, Hooker crossed the Rappahannock and the Rapidan. Because he had divided his forces and could not bring them into battle at the right place he was badly mauled by Lee at Chancellorsville. On May 6 came a dispatch that Hooker had retreated across the Rappahannock. With head bent and hands clasped behind him, Lincoln paced the floor, saying, "My God! My God! What will the country say? What *will* the country say?"

Lee soon crossed upriver and lunged across the Potomac into Maryland toward Pennsylvania. Panic broke out in the North. In a huff Hooker resigned almost on the eve of battle. Lincoln, ignoring cries for the return of McClellan, placed General George Gordon Meade in charge, the fifth general to command in the East within a year. The climactic battle of Gettysburg was joined on July 1 and continued with staggering losses on both sides for the next two days. On July 4 at 10 A.M. Lincoln announced to the country a bloody victory for the North with the wish "that on this day, He whose will, not ours, should be forever done, be everywhere remembered and reverenced with profoundest gratitude."[3]

Within a few days he learned that Vicksburg had fallen to Grant on Independence Day. On July 15, 1863, Lincoln issued a Proclamation of Thanksgiving for these Union victories, acknowledging also the mourning of the nation for the lost. "It is meet and right to recognize and confess the presence of the Almighty Father and the power of His Hand equally in these triumphs and in these sorrows."

The text contains a moving invocation of the Holy Spirit as he called upon the people to "render the homage due to the Divine Majesty, for the wonderful things He has done in the Nation's behalf, and invoke the influence of His Holy Spirit to subdue the anger, which has produced, and so long sustained a needless and cruel rebellion, to change the hearts of the insurgents, to guide the counsels of the Government with wisdom adequate to so great a national emergency, and to visit with tender care and consolation throughout the length and breadth of our land all those who, through the vicissitudes of marches, voyages, battles, and sieges, have been brought to suffer in mind, body, or estate, and finally to lead the whole nation, through the paths of repentance and submission to the Divine Will, back to the perfect enjoyment of Union and fraternal peace."[4]

During the next two months Copperhead activity rose to a peak in the North. Ohio Democrats nominated for governor Clement Vallandigham, who had been arrested by the military and deported to the South, but who now from a base in Canada urged that peace be concluded with the Confederates. A noisy "peace" meeting denouncing Lincoln's "tyranny" was staged in Springfield, Illinois.

To counter this demonstration the Republicans of Illinois campaigned as the National Union party, inviting all loyal Democrats to join them. This fusion group planned a meeting for September 3 in Springfield and invited the President to address them. Unable to be present because of the press of affairs, Lincoln wrote an important letter to his friend James C. Conkling to be read at the Union rally.

Lincoln expressed gratitude for the support of all Union-loving men and justified his military pressure on the South as the only practical means of restoring the Union. He argued that in the eyes of his military commanders emancipation constituted the heaviest blow yet dealt to the rebellion.

"The signs look better. The Father of Waters again goes unvexed to the sea. . . . It is hard to say that anything has been more bravely, and well done, than at Antietam, Murfreesboro, Gettysburg, and on many fields of lesser note. Nor must Uncle Sam's web-feet be forgotten. At all the watery margins they have been present. Not only on the deep sea, the broad bay, and the rapid river, but also up the narrow muddy bayou, and wherever the ground was a little damp, they have been, and made their tracks. Thanks to all. For the great republic—for the principle it lives by, and keeps alive—for man's vast future,— thanks to all."

Here again was the theme of "this nation, under God" with its democratic principles as "the last, best hope of earth." One can almost sense the coming of the Gettysburg Address. Lincoln went on to say that peace "does not appear so distant as it did.

"Still let us not be over-sanguine of a speedy final triumph. Let us be quite sober. Let us diligently apply the means, never doubting that a just God, in His own good time, will give us the rightful result."[5]

One of the notes that rings through this letter is thanksgiving for the hard work and sacrifice of the people. It was said of Lincoln that whenever he was congratulated on a Union victory he always spoke at once of the men who by fighting and dying had actually won it. Once an officer reported to him about conditions among the freedmen on the North Carolina coast, telling of a patriarch who told his people: "Massa Linkum, he eberywhar. He know eberyting. He walk de earf like de Lord!" Lincoln did not smile, but after walking around a bit in silence he remarked: "It is a momentous thing to be the instrument, under Providence, of the liberation of a race."[6]

The note of gratitude was a marked characteristic of Lincoln. He knew how to say thank you to men and to offer praise to God. It was therefore entirely natural that he should accept the suggestion of Sarah Hale and make Thanksgiving a national holiday. Succeeding Presidents have followed the precedent established by him in 1863 and fixed the November date by proclamation. The mood of thankfulness revealed in the Conkling letter found a more solemn and liturgical expression in the official proclamation.

"The year that is drawing towards its close, has been filled with the blessings of fruitful fields and healthful skies. To these bounties, which are so constantly enjoyed that we are prone to forget the source from which they come, others have been added, which are of so extraordinary a nature, that they cannot fail to penetrate and soften even the heart which is habitually insensible to the ever watchful providence of Almighty God."

Lincoln spoke of the maintenance of peace with other countries and the advance of the armed forces. Then in vivid, concrete imagery he summed up the growth of the nation and its expectation.

"Needful diversions of wealth and of strength from the fields of peaceful industry to the national defense, have not arrested the plough, the shuttle or the ship; the axe has enlarged the borders of our settlements, and the mines, as well of iron and coal as of the precious metals, have yielded even more abundantly than heretofore. Population has steadily increased, notwithstanding the waste that has been made in the camp, the siege and the battlefield; and the country, rejoicing in the consciousness of augumented strength and vigor, is permitted to expect continuance of years with large increase of freedom."

Then Lincoln provided the theological interpretation of the nation's situation.

"No human counsel hath devised nor hath any mortal hand worked out these great things. They are the gracious gifts of the Most High God, who, while dealing with us in anger for our sins, hath nevertheless remembered mercy. It has seemed to me fit and proper that they should be solemnly, reverently and gratefully acknowledged as with one heart and one voice by the whole American People."

Lincoln then named the last Thursday in November as "a day

of Thanksgiving and Praise to our beneficent Father who dwelleth in the Heavens." He asked the people to commend "to His tender care all those who have become widows, orphans, mourners or sufferers in the lamentable civil strife in which we are unavoidably engaged, and fervently implore the interposition of the Almighty Hand to heal the wounds of the nation and to restore it as soon as may be consistent with the Divine purposes to the full enjoyment of peace, harmony, tranquillity and Union."[7]

The next significant document of 1863 was of course the Gettysburg Address. It followed naturally upon the Thanksgiving Proclamation. Lord Curzon ranked it and the Second Inaugural as two of the three greatest examples of eloquence in the English language. Edward Everett, whose task it had been to deliver a two-hour oration preceding the President's remarks, recognized it as a jewel. He wrote Lincoln shortly after the dedication of the cemetery, wishing that he might have been able to come as near to the central idea of the occasion in two hours as the President had in two minutes.

Some commentators have dismissed the religious implications of the address by pointing out that there are no biblical quotations in it and that the phrase "under God" was an afterthought. It would be difficult to make a more superficial comment. While it is technically true that there are no texts from Scripture in it, the language is at times biblical and the solemn style has the cadences of the King James Version.

"Four score and seven years ago" is an inspired adaptation of Old Testament counting. The image of the birth of the nation is expressed in the verb "brought forth" borrowed from the common biblical phrase: "she brought forth a son." "The new birth," or the image of biblical regeneration, is the controlling concept behind the picture of purposeful sacrifice—"that this nation, under God, shall have a new birth of freedom." The first and second drafts of his address and the transcriptions of the reporters present show that he must have added the phrase "under God" as he spoke. In the three subsequent copies Lincoln included this inspired addition of his.

But this discussion of its affinities with the language and style of Scripture only begins to scratch the surface of its true religious depth. The central image behind the whole speech is the rite of baptism or the solemn dedication of children to God. The New Testament describes baptism as a dying to sin with Christ in his death and as a rising to newness of life in the power of his resurrection. Lincoln conflates the themes of the life of man in birth, baptismal dedication, and spiritual rebirth with the experience of the nation in its eighty-seven years of history.

Although founded on the proposition that all men are created equal, the nation had denied its universal dedication by narrowing "all" to "all white men." At Gettysburg the old man of sin died that the nation might be reborn in the truth of a growing democracy for all men everywhere.

Basler comments on the Address: "To it he brought the fervor of devoutly religious belief. Democracy was to Lincoln a religion, and he wanted it to be in a real sense the religion of his audience. Thus he combined an elegiac theme with a patriotic theme, skillfully blending the hope of eternal life with the hope of eternal democracy."[8]

His use of the word "proposition" has sometimes been questioned. It has been said that Matthew Arnold read no further. Here of course the image is a proposition in Euclidean geometry that requires proof. Lincoln is supposed to have carried a copy of Euclid with him on the circuit and to have laughingly approved the suggestion of a clergyman to have the Tract Society print the Greek geometrician. The verb "testing" further depicts this process of demonstration although it takes on the overtones of a test of faith such as Abraham's or Job's in the Old Testament. For Lincoln the truth that all men are created equal was not a static concept predicated upon the base of self-evidence.

Here was a basic difference in emphasis between Jefferson and Lincoln. For Jefferson the phrase was a geometrical *axiom* needing no proof, but resting on the basis of "a self-evident truth." For Lincoln in his maturer years the phrase was a *proposition* that was in continual process of being demonstrated. Lincoln's way of rooting democracy in the will of God made it a dynamic faith to live by. The Civil War was "a test" or "trial" of that faith. The theme of being justified by faith, an echo of the Puritan religious inheritance, is also in the background of this language about the testing of a proposition.

The religious images behind the Gettysburg Address are all of one piece with Lincoln's deepened sense of consecration at this time. Some of this evidence has already been pointed out. He told General Sickles that in the crisis of the battle he made a solemn vow that if God would stand by the soldiers he would stand by Him. He told the Baltimore Presbyterians that he wished he was a "more devout" man. The Gettysburg Address partly articulates this "increased devotion" in Lincoln himself as he summons the nation to a higher dedication of its life.

"Four score and seven years ago our fathers brought forth on this continent, a new nation, conceived in Liberty, and dedicated to the proposition that all men are created equal.

"Now we are engaged in a great civil war, testing whether that nation, or any nation so conceived and so dedicated, can long endure. We are met on a great battle-field of that war. We have come to dedicate a portion of that field, as a final resting place for those who here gave their lives that that nation might live. It is altogether fitting and proper that we should do this.

"But, in a larger sense, we can not dedicate—we can not consecrate—we can not hallow—this ground. The brave men, living and dead, who struggled here, have consecrated it, far above our poor power to add or detract. The world will little note, nor long remember what we say here, but it can never forget what they did here. It is for us the living, rather, to be dedicated here to the unfinished work which they who fought here have thus far so nobly advanced. It is for us the living, rather, to be here dedicated to the great task remaining before us—that from these honored dead we take increased devotion to that cause for which they gave the last full measure of devotion—that we here highly resolve that these dead shall not have died in vain—that this nation, under God, shall have a new birth of freedom—and that government of the people, by the people, for the people, shall not perish from the earth."[9]

1864–65—"With Malice toward None,
With Charity for All,
With Firmness in the Right"

Chapter 10

Lincoln continued to feel a personal responsibility for the problem of slavery. The institution affronted his deepest religious and moral convictions and contradicted his understanding of American destiny. Yet his own power to deal with the evil was limited by his responsibilities as a President under oath to uphold the Constitution and to public opinion as a representative leader of the nation. By an "act of military necessity" he had forever freed the slaves in those areas of the Confederacy at war with the United States on January 1, 1863. It left unsolved, of course, the problem of slavery in the border states and in certain areas of the Confederacy already pacified by military government at the date of the Emancipation Proclamation.

He had urged the Congress in his Annual Message of December 1862 to pass constitutional amendments looking toward federal compensation for those states that undertook gradual emancipation. He had assembled the congressional delegations from the border states and pleaded with them to work for state emancipation. He had written many letters to influential men in those states, urging them to mold public opinion in a way favorable to this work. The response to Lincoln's initiative, however, had been meager.

Lincoln finally decided that the only way out of the impasse was congressional initiative for a constitutional amendment, to be ratified by the states, that would forever abolish slavery from the Union. On April 8, 1864, such an amendment passed the Senate, but then failed in the House to secure the necessary two-thirds vote. He suggested that this amendment be incorporated in the Republican platform at the Baltimore convention. This was accordingly done.

In his Annual Message of December 6, 1864, he recommended another vote on the measure, arguing that the results of the fall election showed that in the next Congress the amendment would pass. Since this was inevitable he urged the present Congress to pass the amendment so that the states might the earlier receive the proposed change and begin the process of ratification or rejection.

"It is the voice of the people now, for the first time, heard upon the question. In a great national crisis, like ours, unanimity of action among those seeking a common end is very desirable—almost indispensable. And yet no approach to such unanimity is attainable, unless some deference shall be paid to the will of the majority, simply because it is the will of the majority. In this case the common end is the maintenance of the Union; and, among the means to secure that end, such will, through the election, is most clearly declared in favor of such constitutional amendment."[1]

Lincoln was not, however, content to rest his case on the persuasion of statesmanship alone, where it would have been precarious in the extreme. He showed himself once again the astute politician who had won himself a reputation for log-rolling in the Illinois legislature. He determined to win the needful Democratic votes by promising the patronage that was his to give. One Democratic congressman was to receive a federal appointment for his brother. Another whose election was contested was promised support. In a dramatic roll-call vote before packed galleries the amendment passed by four votes. It was then submitted to the states to become finally the Thirteenth Amendment prohibiting slavery.

Charles A. Dana, who had once been the President's agent in lining up votes for the admission of Nevada to the Union, described Lincoln's prowess: "[He] was a supreme politician. He understood politics because he understood human nature . . . there was no flabby philanthropy about Abraham Lincoln. He was all solid, hard, keen intelligence combined with goodness."[2]

There are two interesting documents that bring out the religious overtones of Lincoln's action during this period just surveyed. One is a letter to Albert Hodges, editor of the Frankfort (Kentucky) *Commonwealth*. It summarized Lincoln's conversation with a Kentucky delegation that had protested the enlisting of Negroes as soldiers. Many of its points anticipated the Second Inaugural and re-emphasized his faith in God's immediate control of the events of history and in His purpose to accomplish justice. Lincoln often repeated the adage about man as proposing, but God as disposing.

"I am naturally anti-slavery. If slavery is not wrong, nothing is wrong. I cannot remember when I did not so think, and feel. And yet I have never understood that the Presidency conferred upon me an unrestricted right to act officially upon this judgment and feeling. . . . I have done no official act in mere deference to my abstract judgment and feeling on slavery. . . .

"I add a word which was not in the verbal conversation. In telling this tale I attempt no compliment to my own sagacity. I claim not to have controlled events, but confess plainly that events have controlled me. Now, at the end of three years' struggle the nation's condition is not what either party, or any man devised, or expected. God alone can claim it. Whither it is tending seems plain. If God now wills the removal of a great wrong, and wills also that we of the North, as well as you of the South, shall pay fairly for our complicity in that wrong, impartial history will find therein new cause to attest and revere the justice and goodness of God."[3]

The second document was a response to a delegation of the American Baptist Home Missionary Society. It had called upon him to present a series of resolutions supporting Lincoln's stand and apparently favoring the end of all slavery. His written reply two days later is about as sharp a criticism of Southern Christians as he ever made, tempered at the end by the Savior's warning on judgment.

Evidence has already been presented that he preferred in his later years to express his objection to slavery in terms of a biblical understanding of work rather than in his earlier derivation of it from the "self-evident truths" of creation. Lincoln felt strongly about the essential importance of labor to society and liked to make it concrete by referring to the injunction on work in Genesis. He had known in early life what it meant to earn bread in the sweat of his brow. He was offended by the arrogant complacency of the planter interests and especially by their mouthpieces in the clergy. To him slavery was a form of stealing. He exposed its pretense by invoking the Golden Rule of the Savior. The passage breathed the passion of an Amos against hypocrisy and injustice, but it was redeemed from sheer denunciation by a Christian perspective on the self and judgment.

". . . I can only thank you for thus adding to the effective and almost unanimous support which the Christian communities are so zealously giving to the country, and to liberty. Indeed it is difficult to conceive how it could be otherwise with anyone professing Christianity, or even having ordinary perceptions of right and wrong. To read in the Bible, as the word of God himself, that 'In the sweat of *thy* face thou shalt eat bread,' and to preach therefrom that, 'In the sweat of *other men's* faces shalt thou eat bread,' to my mind can scarcely be reconciled with honest sincerity. When brought to my final reckoning, may I have to answer for robbing no man of his goods; yet more tolerable even this, than for robbing one of himself, and all that was his. When, a year or two ago, those professedly holy men of the South, met in semblance of prayer and devotion, and, in the Name of Him who said, 'As ye would all men should do unto you, do ye even so unto them,' appealed to the Christian world to aid them in doing to a whole race of men, as they would have no man do unto themselves, to my thinking, they contemned and insulted God and His church, far more than did Satan when he tempted the Savior with the Kingdoms of the earth. The devil's attempt was no more false, and far less hypocritical. But let me forbear, remembering it is also written 'Judge not, lest ye be judged.' "[4]

In the last of his Thanksgiving Day proclamations Lincoln repeated the motifs which are now thoroughly familiar to the reader—the nation devoted to a cause larger than its own life, gratefulness in concrete detail for special providences, penitence as the proper approach of man to God, and the vocation of the American people in the new promised land. There is, however, no dull repetition about the document, for he succeeded in saying it with freshness and in a poetic style that drew both imagery and rhythm from the Bible.

"It has pleased Almighty God to prolong our national life another year, defending us with his guardian care against unfriendly designs from abroad, and vouchsafing to us in His mercy many and signal victories over the enemy, who is of our own household. It has also pleased our Heavenly Father to favor as well our citizens in their homes as our soldiers in their camps and our sailors on the rivers and seas with unusual health. He has largely augmented our free population by emancipation and by immigration, while He has opened to us new sources of wealth, and has crowned the labor of our workingmen in every department of industry with abundant rewards. Moreover, He has been pleased to animate and inspire our minds and hearts with fortitude, courage and resolution sufficient for the great trial of civil war into which we have been brought by our adherence as a nation to the cause of Freedom and Humanity, and to afford us reasonable hopes of an ultimate and happy deliverance from all dangers and afflictions."

He then designated the last Thursday in November as "a day of Thanksgiving and Praise to Almighty God, the beneficent Creator and Ruler of the Universe. And I do farther recommend to my fellow citizens aforesaid that on that occasion they do reverently humble themselves in the dust and from thence offer up penitent and fervent prayers and supplications to the Great Disposer of events for a return of the inestimable blessings of Peace, Union and Harmony throughout the land, which it has pleased Him to assign as a dwelling place for ourselves and for our posterity throughout all generations."[5]

One of the elements of perennial newness in Lincoln's statements about God is the abundant wealth of his titles and attributes in describing the Creator. They can all be summarized under a phrase in his Second Inaugural, "believers in a Living God." For Lincoln the "givenness" of God and God's nearness to him in immediate relationship called forth a tribute of poetic praise. Mrs. Lincoln spoke of his religion as poetry. The devout St. Francis, who sang "The Canticle to the Sun" and imaginatively invested all creation with the breath of personal life, was paralleled by the President, who praised God in a wealth of concrete images. The following list has been selected from the Rutgers edition of his works:

"Almighty, Almighty Architect, Almighty Arm, Almighty Being, Almighty Father, Almighty God, Almighty Hand, Almighty Power, Almighty and Merciful Ruler of the Universe, Beneficent Creator and Ruler of the Universe, Great Disposer of Events, Divine Being, Divine Guidance, Divine Power, Divine Providence, Divine Will, Father, Beneficent Father Who Dwelleth in the Heavens, Common God and Father of All Men, Father in Heaven, Father of Mercies, Great Father of Us All, God of Hosts, God of Right, God of Nations, Most High God, Holy Spirit, Living God, Great and Merciful Maker, Maker of the Universe, Most High, Supreme Being, Supreme Ruler of the Universe."

Any study of Lincoln's religion should examine the practical expression of religious thought and devotion in his everyday life. This is the measuring rod that Lincoln himself used in digging down through the sands of denominationalism to the bedrock of the Savior's life and teaching. Most Christians believe that they should express their love for God by loving their neighbor, but often their religion remains on the level of officially defined concept and piously articulated intention. Lincoln expressed the fruit of Christian living with rare integrity and charm.

Tolstoy was so overwhelmed by this dimension in Lincoln that he could call him "A Christ in miniature." Jesse Fell, in a statement already surveyed, put the matter in a way that compels agreement: ". . . his principles and practices and the spirit of his whole life were of the kind we universally agree to call Christian."

His qualities of forbearance, patience, simple honesty, forgivingness, humility, and kindliness are documented in the stories known to every schoolboy and simply multiplied by his biographers. What Lincoln says about humility and charity rings with a more authentic sound when it is remembered that he could accept calmly the snub of General McClellan in retiring to bed without allowing the waiting President to see him. Its echo rings clearly again in his patient dealing with the vain Chase, who intrigued to get the Republican nomination for himself in 1864.

Lincoln could write in a letter: "I am a patient man—always willing to forgive on the Christian terms of repentance; and also to give ample *time* for repentance."[6] To another correspondent he wrote, "I shall do nothing in malice. What I deal with is too vast for malicious dealing."[7]

From a window of the White House to a group who serenaded him on his re-election, he confessed: "So long as I have been here I have not willingly planted a thorn in any man's bosom. While I am deeply sensible to the high compliment of a reelection; and duly grateful, as I trust, to Almighty God for having directed my countrymen to a right conclusion, as I think, for their own good, it adds nothing to my satisfaction that any other man may be disappointed or pained by the result. May I ask those who have not differed with me, to join with me, in this same spirit towards those who have?"[8]

Lincoln's own spirit of a basic charity toward all men that excluded vindictiveness or malice was expressed in terms of God's will for the whole nation in the Second Inaugural Address. That document with its authentic rootage in a biblical understanding of God, man, and history has become for the whole world a charter of Christian statesmanship. It perfectly expressed the religion of its author, so soon to be struck down, who had said at the Baltimore Sanitary Fair, ". . . I am responsible . . . to the American people, to the Christian world, to history, and on my final account to God."[9]

The address began on a somewhat pedestrian note with Lincoln disclaiming the need for any new statement of policy and summarizing the military situation. Then each new sentence began to mount higher as on eagles' wings.

"Both parties deprecated war; but one of them would *make* war rather than let the nation survive; and the other would *accept* war rather than let it perish. And the war came.

"One eighth of the whole population were colored slaves, not distributed generally over the Union, but localized in the Southern part of it. These slaves constituted a peculiar and powerful interest. All knew that this interest was, somehow, the cause of the war. To strengthen, perpetuate, and extend this interest was the object for which the insurgents would rend the Union, even by war; while the government claimed no right to do more than to restrict the territorial enlargement of it. Neither party expected for the war, the magnitude, or the duration, which it has already attained. Neither anticipated that the *cause* of the conflict might cease with, or even before, the conflict itself should cease. Each looked for an easier triumph, and a result less fundamental and astounding. Both read the same Bible, and pray to the same God; and each invokes His aid against the other. It may seem strange that any men should dare to ask a just God's assistance in wringing their bread from the sweat of other men's faces; but let us judge not that we be not judged. The prayers of both could not be answered; that of neither has been answered fully. The Almighty has His own purposes. 'Woe unto the world because of offenses! For it must needs be that offenses come; but woe to that man by whom the offense cometh!' If we shall suppose that American Slavery is one of those offenses which, in the providence of God, must needs come, but which, having continued through His appointed time, He now wills to remove, and that He gives to both North and South, this terrible war, as the woe due to those by whom the offense came, shall we discern therein any departure from those divine attributes which the believers in a Living God always ascribe to Him? Fondly do we hope—fervently do we pray—that this mighty scourge of war may speedily pass away. Yet, if God wills that it continue, until all the wealth piled by the bond-man's two hundred and fifty years of unrequited toil shall be sunk, and until every drop of blood drawn with the lash, shall be paid with another drawn with the sword, as was said three thousand years ago, so still it must be said 'the judgments of the Lord, are true and righteous altogether.'

"With malice toward none; with charity for all; with firmness in the right, as God gives us to see the right, let us strive on to finish the work we are in; to bind up the nation's wounds; to care for him who shall have borne the battle, and for his widow, and his orphan—to do all which may achieve and cherish a just, and a lasting peace, among ourselves, and with all nations."[10]

Comment on this address seems almost blasphemous, but it may be helpful to see it as the climax of Lincoln's religious development. Earlier, in the proclamation after Bull Run, he had urged the nation to see the hand of God in the visitation of war. Increasingly he defined the theological issue in the conflict.

His papers and letters show his belief that God willed "His almost chosen people" like Israel of old to be the bearer of new freedom to all men everywhere. The Puritan background of Lincoln's confidence in American destiny under God had become rationalized in the eighteenth and nineteenth centuries into the dream of world democracy with the original religious perspective rapidly disappearing into the distance.

With his incisive logic Lincoln gave definition to America's hope for democracy in terms compelling to his contemporaries, but he also sustained that vision in its original religious rootage and reference to God's will. The religious interpretation was organic and fundamental. It never savored of a pious but irrelevant afterthought as it does in so much contemporary political and pulpit oratory. The depth of Lincoln's religious interpretation of the nation's history, however, was not merely an inheritance from the past but a living power of rekindled insight.

Lincoln's gift of mystical intuition led him into a specific explanation of the slavery issue in terms of the Old Testament prophets. His Puritan forebears would have called it a "discerning of the signs of the times," a feeling for "particular providences." As Lincoln analyzed God's intention to lead men into larger freedom and appropriated to his use the language of the Declaration of Independence and the sayings of the Founding Fathers he came in the context of events to regard slavery as a contradiction of God's will. This defiance of God's justice had been built into the life of the nation and was therefore subject to God's judgment.

The long, unhappy debates over the slavery issue had weakened the nation and made it seem hypocritical to aspiring men in other countries. For somewhat more than the last year of his life Lincoln understood the tragedy and suffering of the Civil War as God's judgment upon this evil and as punishment to bring about its removal. The judgment fell upon both sides, for slavery was a national and not merely a sectional evil. The North had also prospered from the cheap raw materials that slave labor fed into its factories. It was conceivable to Lincoln that a just God might allow the war to continue "until all the wealth piled by the bond-man's two hundred and fifty years of unrequited toil shall be sunk." In the severe language of Scripture Lincoln held the nation under judgment: "the judgments of the Lord are true and righteous altogether."

But the judgments of God have as their purpose the reformation of His people. The renewal of an America newly dedicated to the increase of freedom had been his theme at Gettysburg and must be understood as the implied correlative here of the emphasis upon judgment.

The leaven of Christianity that is at work in this address and carries the analysis of judgment beyond that of an Amos or a Jeremiah is expressed in the Savior's warning about the peril of passing judgment. It is also present in the almost scriptural paraphrase of the Savior's summary of the law and of St. Paul's famous chapter on love that Lincoln achieves in his phrases "With malice toward none; with charity for all." The disclaimer of human judgments on the opponent does not lead, however, to irresolution in action. The very opposite is the case. Understanding the perspective of two antagonists before the judgment seat of God and thereby freed from the tyranny of self-righteous fanaticism, there comes to Lincoln the resource of "firmness in the right, as God gives us to see the right."

This document is one of the most astute pieces of Christian theology ever written. It is also a charter of Christian ethics. It may seem strange to call Lincoln a theologian, for he was obviously not one in any technical sense. There are many profundities in the Christian religion which he never did illuminate, but in the area of his vision he saw more keenly than anyone since the inspired writers of the Bible. He knew he stood under the living God of history.

He understood, for example, the finiteness of man's religious perspective without thereby becoming either a relativist or a skeptic. He achieved a religious perspective above partisan strife that was not shared by most of the Christian theologians of his day or any day, who often express Christian insights in obsolete terms in a way that ultimately deifies the position of man. Lincoln could detach himself from his own interested participation in events and submit all, including himself as judging, to higher judgment. The highly tentative nature of his own judgments do not argue uncertainty or irresolution but simply confess that God is God and man remains on every level man. The utter priority and "givenness" of God had for Lincoln as its corollary the utter dependence of man upon God.

The Second Inaugural illuminates the finiteness of man when in sincerity men embrace opposite courses of action under the conviction that each is responsive to God's will. "Both read the same Bible, and pray to the same God; and each invokes His aid against the other." It has often been pointed out that religion has exacerbated human strife by clothing diametrically opposite lines of activity with the sanctions of absolute holiness.

There is a fanaticism in many people that blinds them to the truth of their position, increases their self-righteousness, and isolates them from their fellows. It is the fallacy of supposing that a sincere intention to do God's will guarantees that what I sincerely do is the will of God. Lincoln could detach himself from the element of pretense in the idealistic claims made by both sides. In his meditation on the divine will Lincoln opened up horizons beyond the simple but all too common analysis— that one side is right and the other is wrong. Both could not be right. Each might be partly right and partly wrong and God might use both sides as His instruments to effect a result not foreseen by either side. Lincoln argued that this was the case with the Civil War. "Only God can claim it," he once said, thereby stating that the complexities of historical events are so involved that finite man cannot claim infallible insight for his own interpretations. Lincoln expressed this again in his own comments on the Second Inaugural in a letter written to Thurlow Weed:

"I expect the latter to wear as well as—perhaps better than—anything I have produced; but I believe it is not immediately popular. Men are not flattered by being shown that there has been a difference of purpose between the Almighty and them. To deny it, however, in this case, is to deny that there is a God governing the world. It is a truth which I thought needed to be told; and as whatever of humiliation there is in it, falls most directly on myself, I thought others might afford for me to tell it."[11]

The fact, however, that the divine will remains in the

realm of ultimate mystery need not lead to a despairing or resigned agnosticism. Because Lincoln was aware that Providence would overrule the element of pretension in the highly idealistic claims made by each side he was not therefore led to the conclusion that responsible action undertaken by either side would necessarily be irrelevant to the moral issue. The mystery is illuminated by meaning like lightning in the night sky. Knowing that God and not Lincoln would have the final word in the dilemma of the two contestants at prayer, he could yet venture provisional judgments and act resolutely in their light. "It may seem strange that any men should dare to ask a just God's assistance in wringing their bread from the sweat of other men's faces . . . let us strive on to finish the work we are in." Lincoln's sympathy for the dilemma of the Quakers, caught between pacificism and emancipation as an act in war, is another illustration of the depth of his biblical spirituality on this point.

He could appreciate the sincerity of his foe although he believed him wrong, but because of his religious perspective he could deal magnanimously and forgivingly without the self-righteousness of the victor. This point of vantage beyond the strife of factions did not, however, kill the nerve of resolution. Since God was supreme a man might act without fanaticism and hatred on the one hand and without torturing doubt or irresolution on the other.

This is the charter of responsible action for the Christian citizen. St. Francis, the loving, gentle imitator of Christ, will always be dear to the hearts of men. The appeal, however, of the ascetic who leaves the responsibilities of society for the cultivation of individual piety and ecstatic person-to-person relationships has an element of romanticism in it. Lincoln represents the responsible Christian citizen of this world struggling to be responsive to the guidance of God amid the challenges of the full historic setting of man's life. Both the Christian saint and the Christian statesman are needed, but there can be little doubt as to which one more fully represents the demands of a God revealed through the Bible as the "Great Disposer of Events."

Lincoln's religious analysis of the nation's history is as relevant today as it was when he painfully developed it. One has only to substitute the phrase "segregation in public education" for Lincoln's word "slavery" and his theological analysis becomes luminous. America stands today among the nations of the world as the self-proclaimed defender of democracy in areas that are being progressively inundated by totalitarianism. Our professed defense of the right of all men everywhere to be free sounds increasingly hollow to multitudes in Asia and Africa because of our racial discrimination at home. If the rising colored peoples of the world turn from democracy to communism partly because of our racialism the security of America will become a very frail thing. And yet "the judgments of the Lord are true and righteous altogether."

In our competition with the Soviet Union we proclaim ourselves the defenders of religion against atheistic materialism, but if infatuation with our own materialist standard of living makes us unwilling to use our resources to lift the economy of less developed nations we may find ourselves without friends in a world increasingly dominated by communism.

Yet "the judgments of the Lord are true and righteous altogether."

To a religious understanding of the nation's destiny that is as meaningful today as for the crisis of the Civil War Lincoln adds a dynamic for responsible action that is equally helpful. Courageous action prayerfully undertaken in openness and in unself-righteous concern for all men is the leaven that can alter the whole lump. Commenting on Lincoln's religious insights into the moral dilemmas of his day, Reinhold Niebuhr in his *Irony of American History* writes as follows:

"This combination of moral resoluteness about the immediate issues with a religious awareness of another dimension of meaning and judgment must be regarded as almost a perfect model of the difficult but not impossible task of remaining loyal and responsible toward the moral treasures of a free civilization on the one hand while yet having some religious vantage point over the struggle."[12]

It was such a perspective that enabled Lincoln not only to serve the Union without self-righteous stances but also, therefore, to serve it more effectively. Those who wield great power are often snared in traps of their own making when they become blinded by considerations of prestige.

Lincoln could concentrate on practical actions needed to restore the Union because he was free of the Radical Republican determination to punish the South and rationalize its own ideology of the war. Christian statesmanship marks the address he made on the evening of April 11, 1865, his last public utterance. He appealed to the people to support his principles and action for reconstruction.

"We all agree that the seceded States, so called, are out of their proper practical relation with the Union; and that the sole object of the government, civil and military, in regard to those States is to again get them into that proper practical relation. I believe it is not only possible, but in fact, easier, to do this, without deciding, or even considering, whether these States have even been out of the Union, than with it. Finding themselves safely at home, it would be utterly immaterial whether they had ever been abroad. Let us all join in doing the acts necessary to restoring the proper practical relations between these States and the Union; and *each forever after, innocently indulge his own opinion* whether, in doing the acts, he brought the States from without, into the Union, or only gave them proper assistance, they never having been out of it."[13]

The problems of national reconciliation in a spirit of forgiveness were uppermost in his mind when the bullet struck him on Good Friday. He carried to his death another item of unfinished business mentioned four days before in this last speech. "He, from whom all blessings flow, must not be forgotten. A call for a national thanksgiving is being prepared, and will be duly promulgated."[14]

Any study of Lincoln's religion should lead to some brief characterization of his position. Since his religious development was a continuing process there is always danger of freezing prematurely upon some formula which then becomes a caricature. Dodge has pointed to the slow maturing of his literary style. Others have traced the gradual evolution of his views on slavery. Judging by the acceleration noticeable in his last years it would be folly to assume that he had reached his religious maturity when the assassin's bullet cut short his earthly span.

Francis Grierson in his deeply moving *The Valley of the Shadows* characterized Lincoln as a "practical mystic." Many have been content to stop here, although the word "mystic" demands further definition.

Nathaniel Stephenson concluded that "his religion continues to resist intellectual formulation. He never accepted any definite creed. To the problems of theology, he applied the same sort of reasoning that he applied to the problems of the law. He made a distinction, satisfactory to himself at least, between the essential and incidental, and rejected everything that did not seem to him altogether essential."[15] Granting the deeply personal and individual character of Lincoln's religion, is it possible to give a more precise description than this?

Lincoln was unquestionably our most religious President. Professor Randall concluded the fourth volume of his great study with a chapter entitled "God's Man." "Lincoln was a man of more intense religiosity than any other President the United States ever had. . . . Surely, among successful American politicians, Lincoln is unique in the way he breathed the spirit of Christ while disregarding the letter of Christian doctrine. And the letter killeth, but the spirit giveth life."[16]

Randall's judgment was anticipated by a number of Lincoln's contemporaries. Henry Whitney, his circuit-riding friend, wrote: "The conclusion is inevitable, that Mr. Lincoln was practically and essentially, though not ritualistically a Christian."[17] Isaac Arnold, congressman from Illinois and a close friend, shared the same estimate: "No more reverent Christian than he ever sat in the executive chair. . . . It is not claimed that he was orthodox. For creeds and dogmas he cared little. But in the great fundamental principles of religion, of the Christian religion, he was a firm believer."[18]

There is some evidence that Lincoln may have been considering membership in the church. His friend Noah Brooks, who was to have become his secretary, made this point. "In many conversations with him, I absorbed the firm conviction that Mr. Lincoln was at heart a Christian man, believed in the Savior, and was seriously considering the step which would formally connect him with the visible Church on earth."[19] In the light of Lincoln's unorthodox attitude on universal salvation and his distaste for creedal definitions it is not likely that he would have sought membership in the Washington church which he was attending. Considering the vow which he made before the battle of Gettysburg, the weight of evidence points more toward Lincoln's feeling a concern to make a public confession of his faith rather than to seek membership in any one church.[20]

By the creedal standards of the churches of his day he was not "an orthodox Christian." His wife said that he was not "a technical Christian." Our definition today is a more liberal one. David Mearns has aptly called him a "Christian without a Creed."[21] This may be the least inadequate phrase. It would, however, be a serious mistake to interpret it to mean that his faith was without specific content.

A better phrase might be "a biblical Christian." It would at once shift the emphasis from the institutional side of Christianity, in which his religion was defective, to its bedrock foundation in Scripture. From the Bible in a quite independent way he quarried granite to support a religious interpretation of American history and of man's vast future.

To use a still more precise definition, Lincoln was "a biblical prophet" who saw himself as "an instrument of God" and his country as God's "almost chosen people" called to world responsibility.

In *The Soul of Abraham Lincoln* William Barton reported his ownership of a half page of note paper in Lincoln's handwriting. On it Lincoln had copied out, presumably for his own meditation, a passage from the Puritan theologian, Richard Baxter. The passage was about man's assurance of salvation. That assurance was grounded not in man's subjective feelings but in the sense of direction to his life. These wise words may have spoken to Lincoln's understanding of his own religious situation:

"It is more pleasing to God to see his people study Him and His will directly, than to spend the first and chief of their effort about attaining comfort [i.e., assurance of belief] for themselves. We have faith given us, principally that we might believe and live by it in daily applications of Christ. You may believe immediately (by God's help), but getting assurance of it may be the work of a great part of your life."[22]

Appendix I

In 1920, William Barton concluded *The Soul of Abraham Lincoln* with a creed expressed entirely in Lincoln's own words with only slight changes for grammatical reasons. It is printed here as a classic tour de force in studies of Lincoln's religion. Its danger is that, separated from its context in his life and writings, it overemphasizes the doctrinal element. He did, after all, protest against complicated creeds as requirements for church membership. Its strength, however, is to underscore the biblically rooted faith of the man in opposition to recent interpretations of his religion as "creedless" in the sense of being "wholly free from any doctrinal commitment."

The Creed of Abraham Lincoln in His Own Words

I believe in God, the Almighty Ruler of Nations, our great and good and merciful Maker, our Father in Heaven, who notes the fall of a sparrow, and numbers the hairs of our heads.

I believe in His eternal truth and justice.

I recognize the sublime truth announced in the Holy Scriptures and proven by all history that those nations only are blest whose God is the Lord.

I believe that it is the duty of nations as well as of men to own their dependence upon the overruling power of God, and to invoke the influence of His Holy Spirit; to confess their sins and transgressions in humble sorrow, yet with assured hope that genuine repentance will lead to mercy and pardon.

I believe that it is meet and right to recognize and confess the presence of the Almighty Father equally in our triumphs and in those sorrows which we may justly fear are a punishment inflicted upon us for our presumptuous sins to the needful end of our reformation.

I believe that the Bible is the best gift which God has ever given to men. All the good from the Saviour of the world is communicated to us through this book.

I believe the will of God prevails. Without Him all human reliance is vain. Without the assistance of that Divine Being, I cannot succeed. With that assistance I cannot fail.

Being a humble instrument in the hands of our Heavenly Father, I desire that all my works and acts may be according to His will; and that it may be so, I give thanks to the Almighty, and seek His aid.

I have a solemn oath registered in heaven to finish the work I am in, in full view of my responsibility to my God, with malice toward none; with charity for all; with firmness in the right as God gives me to see the right. Commending those who love me to His care, as I hope in their prayers they will commend me, I look through the help of God to a joyous meeting with many loved ones gone before.

Appendix II

Jay Monaghan's *A Lincoln Bibliography, 1839–1939* listed nearly four thousand books and pamphlets on Lincoln. The output has not slackened in the last two decades. The Library of Congress catalogues about fifty items on Lincoln's religion. The aim of the following list is to winnow the chaff from the grain and present some suggestions to beginners in this vast field.

Lincoln's religion should be studied as part of his life. The best one-volume study representing current Lincoln scholarship is Benjamin Thomas's *Abraham Lincoln* (1952). While it predates critical Lincoln studies, Lord Charnwood's *Abraham Lincoln* (1917) is most valuable for its analysis of his character and of his significance as a world figure.

Beyond the one-volume scope the reader has interesting choices. He may select the ten-volume *Abraham Lincoln: A History* by Nicolay and Hay (1890). Because it was written by Lincoln's private secretaries and was submitted for approval to Robert Lincoln, the President's son, it has often been called the "official" biography. It has by no means been replaced by later studies. It is not, however, particularly perceptive on the subject of Lincoln's faith.

Carl Sandburg's two-volume *Prairie Years* (1926) and the four-volume *War Years* (1939) constitute an artistic masterpiece and should become an American classic. Filled with local color and the flavor of the times, Sandburg's books show a lively interest in Lincoln's religion. His good chapter of Lincoln's laughter and religion has been mentioned previously. In 1954, Sandburg published a one-volume condensation of his work.

James Randall's four-volume study, *Lincoln the President* (1955) is the work of a gifted writer and a professional historian. It is a needed corrective to the mythical picture of Lincoln that underlay so many older studies of his religion. Professor Randall's chapter on "God's Man" shows an appreciative interest in Lincoln's faith, but it is not integrated with the larger study itself in a way that would bring out the developmental aspect of Lincoln's religion. Professor Richard Current has edited Randall's writings to produce *Mr. Lincoln* (1957), a one-volume concentration on Lincoln the man.

Professor Allan Nevins's four-volume *Ordeal of the Union* (1947) and *Emergence of Lincoln* (1950) are helpful for understanding the history of the United States from 1846 to 1861.

Paul Angle's *A Shelf of Lincoln Books: A Critical, Selective Bibliography of Lincolniana* (1946) is our best introduction to eighty-one books dealing with special Lincoln topics. Benjamin Thomas's *Portrait for Posterity* (1947) studies very interestingly the biographers of Lincoln and outlines briefly their battles over Lincoln's religion.

The basic source for Lincoln's religion must remain the eight-volume edition of his collected works published by Rutgers in 1953 with Roy Basler as editor. Nearly all of the significant material has been reprinted in this book, which the writer has designed as an anthology of Lincoln's writings on religion as well as an interpretation of his religion. Most of the early books failed to understand that Lincoln is a better interpreter of his own faith than either Herndon or Holland ever could be. David Donald's *Lincoln's Herndon* (1948) throws a critical spotlight over secondary and tertiary levels of testimony. Albert House has studied "The

Genesis of the Lincoln Religious Controversy" in *Proceedings of the Middle States Association of History and Social Science Teachers* (1938). A full-length study of all the sources for Lincoln's religion is much needed.

Early works that are still useful would include William Herndon and Jesse Weik, *Herndon's Life of Lincoln,* particularly the edition of 1930 with a critical introduction by Paul Angle. F. B. Carpenter's *Six Months at the White House* (1866) is an extremely valuable source, especially when the artist records his firsthand experiences. Douglas C. McMurtrie in 1936 edited *Lincoln's Religion,* which contains an address by the Rev. James Reed that was first published in *Scribner's* in 1873. It also contains Herndon's answering lecture to Reed, which was first printed in the *State Register of Springfield. Lincoln's Religious Belief,* by B. F. Irwin, was first published in the *Illinois State Journal* May 16, 1874, and may be consulted in Appendix VI to Barton's *Soul of Abraham Lincoln.*

Two twentieth-century studies are worth mentioning. William J. Johnstone, *Abraham Lincoln: The Christian* (1913), is a carefully documented study, but it uses materials in a very naïve way. Its interpretations far outrun the evidence. John Wesley Hill, *Abraham Lincoln, Man of God* (1920), fortunately does not mold his materials as excessively as Johnstone, but the author has uncritically accepted items such as the Lincoln letter of March 2, 1837, to the Rev. James Lemen, now regarded as a forgery.

Two examples of extreme positions are interesting. Ervin Chapman's *Latest Light on Lincoln* (1917) has already been quoted as a representative of the pious school, bordering more on hagiography than history. John E. Remsburg, on the other side, devoted over three hundred pages of his *Six Historic Americans* (1906), which he wrote for the Freethinker press, to a ponderous and shrill argument that Lincoln was once and always an infidel. Remsburg and Herndon corresponded sympathetically on this theme.

The great classic in the field has been William E. Barton's

The Soul of Abraham Lincoln (1920), which has not yet been superseded in its encyclopedic criticism of sources. New materials have, however, come to light and Barton's book has a cluttered aspect that makes it tedious to read. The element of source criticism overwhelms Barton's own interpretation of Lincoln's religion. Its appendices make available a number of useful documents to which reference has already been made.

Edgar DeWitt Jones's *Lincoln and the Preachers* (1948) presents a good survey of just what the title indicates. There is a useful appendix, "Who's Who of the Preachers in the Lincoln Story." H. H. Horner's *The Growth of Lincoln's Faith* (1939) and Ralph Lindstrom's *Lincoln Finds God* (1958) are interesting short interpretations. Clarence Macartney's *Lincoln and the Bible* (1949) is a valuable and interestingly written study.

Other significant books and manuscript sources used in the preparation of this book are mentioned in the footnotes. *Lincoln Lore*, published by the Lincoln National Life Foundation and now edited by Gerald McMurtry, contains interesting material from time to time on the subject of Lincoln's religion.

Reinhard Luthin's *The Real Abraham Lincoln* (1960) is chiefly valuable for its encyclopedic detail and its bibliographical listings. Louis Warren's *Lincoln's Youth: 1816–1830* has helpful background studies of religious movements and clergy in Indiana. *Lincoln Day-By-Day: 1809–1865*, a three volume chronology edited chiefly by Earl Miers and published for the Lincoln Sesquicentennial Commission, is a useful tool. It has (hopefully) dealt a death blow to the Beecher incident discussed in the first chapter.

Appendix III

In spite of Lincoln's statement that he was not a member of any church many zealous denominationalists have claimed Lincoln as a member of their group or as about to become such. Sometimes the errors are honest ones. Nearly every year some newspaper or religious journal repeats this misinformation only to be quoted in the future as an authority on the subject. It is no easy task to trace back these lines to the initial error or overstatement.

Shortly after Herbert Hoover became president a publication claimed both Presidents Lincoln and Hoover as Friends. This error as regards Lincoln may have had its source in the statement in Lincoln's autobiographical sketch for Jesse Fell that some of his ancestors were Quakers.

The statement that Lincoln was once a Roman Catholic has often appeared in print. One of his early teachers, Zachariah Riney, was a Roman Catholic. A rumor that Lincoln was a lapsed Roman Catholic gained some currency about 1860, possibly stemming from Lincoln's having been attorney for Father Chiniquy, who broke dramatically with his church. Cardinal Mundelein of Chicago was reported in the press in 1927 as having said: "When Father St. Cyr came to say mass for Lincoln's stepmother, Mr. Lincoln would prepare the altar himself. Indeed with his own hands Abraham carved out six wooden chairs [candlesticks?] to be used at the mass." Lincoln's aunt Mary Mudd Lincoln and her son Abraham were Roman Catholics. Apparently, someone early confused Lincoln's stepmother, who was never a Roman Catholic, with an aunt who was, and then confused Lincoln's cousin Abraham with the future president himself.

Regularly it is affirmed that Lincoln was a member of the Disciples of Christ. One innocent and likely source is the fact that Lincoln's parents became Disciples after they moved to Illinois. The not so innocent source is the Reverend John O'Kane who stated: "I baptised him in a creek near Springfield . . . I placed his name on the church book. He lived and died a member of the Church of Christ." Lincoln's name is not in the register of the church and the episode must be adjudged sheer fabrication in the light of the President's statement that he was not a church member.

One of the hardier perennials is the statement that Lincoln was a Spiritualist. According to some questionable evidence Lincoln attended some seances. He met several mediums. The whole country was swept at this time by interest in the Spiritualist Movement. Nettie Colburn Maynard's *Was Abraham Lincoln a Spiritualist?*, published in 1891, together with earlier claims and spirit messages alleged to have been arriving ever since, appear to be the "evidence" in point, judging by indignant letters I have received for failing to class Lincoln as a Spiritualist. John Nicolay, Lincoln's private secretary and biographer replied on November 24, 1894, to Jesse Weik, who sought information on this point:

"Yours of November 19 is received. I have not read either of the books you mention, but of course there will be no end to the extravagant stories invented and related about Mr. Lincoln.

"I never knew of his attending a seance of Spiritualists at the White House or elsewhere, and if he ever did so it was out of mere curiosity, and as a matter of pastime, just as you or I would do. That he was in any sense a so-called 'Spiritualist' seems to me almost too absurd to need contradiction."

Dr. R. Gerald McMurtry has surveyed the evidence in the November, 1962, and in the January and February, 1963, issues of *Lincoln Lore.* Jay Monaghan's "Was Abraham Lincoln Really a Spiritualist?", in the *Journal of the Illinois State Historical Society* (June, 1941), presents the analysis of an historian.

The fact that the Foundry Methodist Church in Washington made the President a life director of its missionary society has been stretched at times to imply church membership. The Rev. Edward Watson reported, in the *Christian Advocate* (November 11, 1909) the claim of the Rev. James Jacquess that Lincoln was converted during revivals in 1839 in the Methodist church at Springfield of which he was the pastor.

Dr. Gurley, who was the Lincolns' pastor in Washington at the New York Avenue Presbyterian Church was reported by numerous hearers to have said in his old age that "but for the assassin who took his life [Lincoln] would have made public profession of his faith in Christ on Easter 1865." This claim has been made to me in writing by one of Dr. Gurley's grandsons. This statement must surely be a dramatic overstatement. At any rate, Dr. Gurley made no mention of it in his funeral address on Lincoln.

So numerous have been the claims that Lincoln was a member of the most diverse churches that Louis Warren, surveying some of the evidence in *Lincoln Lore* (February 13, 1956), entitled his article "Lincoln—A Cosmopolitan Christian"!

Notes and References

Chapter 1

1. Francis B. Carpenter, *Six Months at the White House with Abraham Lincoln* (1866), pp. 89–90.

2. Robert B. Warden, *Life of S. P. Chase,* pp. 481–82, quoted in Nicolay and Hay, *Abraham Lincoln: A History* (1890), Vol. VI, pp. 159–60.

3. "The Diary of Gideon Welles," *Atlantic Monthly,* 1909, p. 369.

4. *The Collected Works of Abraham Lincoln* (CWAL, henceforth) (Rutgers University Press, 1953), Vol. V, pp. 388–89. Lincoln's mistakes in spelling, which were properly retained by the Rutgers editors, have been corrected in the quotations to allow the reader to concentrate on the thought. Slight changes have at times been made in punctuation.

5. CWAL, Vol. V, pp. 419–25.

6. Narrated by William Johnstone in *Abraham Lincoln: The Christian* (1913), pp. 91–93. Johnstone interviewed one of the Beecher grandsons in Philadelphia.

7. Ward H. Lamon, *The Life of Abraham Lincoln* (1872), p. 489. Also quoted in Carl Sandburg, *The War Years,* Vol. IV, pp. 244–45. Lincoln's statement that dreams are nowadays seldom told has been corrected with the advent of Freud!

8. Stephen Vincent Benét, *John Brown's Body* (1928), p. 213.

Chapter 2

1. CWAL, Vol. I, p. 1.
2. Ervin Chapman, *Latest Light on Lincoln,* (1917), p. 315.
3. CWAL, Vol. I, p. 386.
4. Lamon, *The Life of Abraham Lincoln,* p. 39.
5. Benjamin Thomas, *Lincoln's New Salem* (1934), p. 89.
6. Benjamin Thomas, in *Portrait for Posterity* (1947), has sketched the battle among Lincoln biographers over his religion. A full-length study of this area is much needed, although the primary data for Lincoln's religion must always remain his own speeches and writings. David Donald's careful study, *Lincoln's Herndon* (1948), has made important contributions to the question of Herndon's reliability on the religious issue. For example, Donald points out that Holland's use of a famous Bateman interview with Lincoln was based on an eight-page letter from Bateman. It did not depend upon Holland's imaginative recollection of a conference with Bateman as Herndon and most Lincoln scholars have supposed. Thomas's evaluation is as follows:

"The controversy over Lincoln's religion seems now to have been a bandying of words. Neither side defined its terms. Had they done so, they might have found they were not too far apart. But, in its later stages, what was originally an honest-if-violent difference of opinion, degenerated into a promotional intrigue with Black [ghost writer of Lamon's *Life of Abraham Lincoln*] the venal prompter and Herndon his gullible stooge" (p. 89).

7. David Donald has a perceptive comment on this debate: "It is a mistake to consider these two main streams of tradition as representing respectively the 'ideal' and the 'real' Lincoln. Each was legendary in character. The conflict in Lincoln biography between the Holland-Hay-Tarbell school and the Herndon-Lamon contingent was not essentially a battle over factual differences; it was more like a religious war. One school portrayed a mythological patron saint; the other, an equally mythological frontier hero. Gradually the two conceptions began to blend" (*Lincoln's Herndon,* p. 372).

8. William Herndon and Jesse Weik, *Herndon's Life of Lincoln* (1949), p. 355. There is a helpful introduction by Paul Angle.

9. Letter from Mentor Graham to B. F. Irwin, March 17, 1874.

10. I Corinthians 15:20–25, 28.

11. Henry Rankin, *Personal Recollections of A. Lincoln* (1916), pp. 324–26. Rankin claimed that his mother's memory was of a high order and that she gave great care to her report of Lincoln's words.

12. CWAL, Vol. I, p. 8.

13. Ibid., p. 75.

Chapter 3

1. Carl Sandburg, *The Prairie Years* (1926), Vol. I, p. 264.

2. CWAL, Vol. I, p. 78.

3. Ibid., pp. 108–15.

4. Ibid., pp. 271–79.

5. Ibid., p. 228.

6. Ibid., p. 229.

7. Ibid., p. 261.

8. Ibid., pp. 267–68.

9. Ibid., p. 282.

10. Ibid., p. 289.

11. Ruth Painter Randall, *The Courtship of Mr. Lincoln* (1957), p. 168. Mrs. Randall published an excellent short article in the New York *Times*, February 7, 1954, entitled "Lincoln's Faith Was Born of Anguish."

12. CWAL, Vol. I, p. 303.

Chapter 4

1. CWAL, Vol. I, p. 320.

2. Sandburg, *The Prairie Years*, Vol. I, pp. 336–37.

3. CWAL, Vol. I, p. 384.

4. Ibid., p. 382.

5. Henry C. Deming, *Eulogy upon Abraham Lincoln before the General Assembly of Connecticut* (1865), p. 42.

6. CWAL, Vol. VII, p. 351.

7. Henry C. Whitney, *Life on the Circuit with Lincoln* (1892), p. 267.

8. *Herndon's Life of Lincoln*, p. 56.

9. CWAL, Vol. V, pp. 403–4.

10. Benjamin Thomas, *Abraham Lincoln*, p. 130.

11. CWAL, Vol. I, p. 368.

12. Ibid., Vol. II, p. 97.

13. *Scribner's Magazine*, July 1873, p. 333.

14. James Smith, *The Christian's Defense* (1843), p. 96.

15. Joshua Speed, *Lecture on Abraham Lincoln*, pp. 32–33.

16. Statement of December 24, 1872, quoted in William Barton, *Soul of Abraham Lincoln* (1920), p. 164.

17. James Smith to Herndon, January 24, 1867, first published in Springfield *Daily Illinois Journal*, March 12, 1867.

18. *Herndon's Life of Lincoln*, p. 354.

19. J. E. Remsburg, *Six Historic Americans* (1906), pp. 114–15.

20. Lamon, *Life of Abraham Lincoln*, pp. 490–92.

Chapter 5

1. Thomas, *Abraham Lincoln*, p. 143.

2. CWAL, Vol. VIII, p. 155.

3. Ibid., Vol. II, pp. 247–83. The Peoria Speech.

4. Ibid., pp. 546–47.

5. Ibid., p. 501.

6. T. Harry Williams, *Selected Writings and Speeches of Abraham Lincoln* (1943), p. xviii, Introduction.

7. CWAL, Vol. III, pp. 204–5.

8. Ibid., Vol. II, pp. 320–23.

9. Ibid., p. 318.

10. Ibid., Vol. III, p. 410.

11. Ibid., p. 462.

12. Letter of Isaac Cogdal to B. F. Irwin, April 10, 1874.

13. Dictated and signed by Jonathan Harnett to B. F. Irwin, and sent by latter to *State Journal*, April 20, 1874.

14. Robert D. Richardson, *Abraham Lincoln's Autobiography* (1947), Pt. II, pp. 33-34.

15. Letter of Mrs. Rebecca R. Pomeroy in *Lincoln Scrapbook,* Library of Congress, p. 54.

16. *Lincoln's Devotional* (1957) was originally entitled *The Believer's Daily Treasure* and published by the Religious Tract Society (London) (1852).

17. CWAL, Vol. III, p. 339.

18. Ibid., Vol. IV, p. 5.

19. Ibid., p. 16.

20. Ibid., pp. 190-91. This version follows the one in Lincoln's and Nicolay's handwriting set down after the event and is the one preferred by the Rutgers's editors. The two alternate versions included by the editors use such terms as "Divine Providence," "Almighty Being," "the great God," "the God of our fathers," and "the same omniscient mind and Almighty arm."

Chapter 6

1. CWAL, Vol. IV, p. 220.

2. Ibid., p. 236.

3. Ibid., pp. 262-71. The First Inaugural.

4. Ibid., p. 482.

5. Ibid., p. 386.

6. Letter of Mrs. Rebecca R. Pomeroy, *Lincoln Scrapbook,* Library of Congress, p. 54.

7. Ida Tarbell, *The Life of Abraham Lincoln* (1902), Vol. II, pp. 89-92. She fails to give enough emphasis to Lincoln's earlier religious awaken-

ing, recorded in his letter to Speed during his broken engagement to Mary Todd.

8. Carpenter, *Six Months at the White House*, pp. 117-19.

9. CWAL, Vol. VIII, p. 117.

10. *Scribner's Monthly*, 1873, p. 343.

11. Letter of Noah Brooks to J. A. Reed, December 31, 1878.

12. William E. Curtis, *The True Abraham Lincoln* (1903), pp. 385-86.

13. James F. Rusling, *Men and Things I Saw in Civil War Days* (1899), p. 15. The description of this incident in Johnstone's *Abraham Lincoln: The Christian*, p. 113, has a facsimile endorsement by General Sickles (February 11, 1911) and by General Rusling (February 17, 1910).

14. Noah Brooks, *Harper's Monthly*. July 1865.

15. CWAL, Vol. V, p. 327.

16. Ibid., Vol. VI, p. 114.

17. Carpenter, op. cit., p. 282.

18. CWAL, Vol. VI, pp. 535-36. Version printed in the Washington *National Republican*. October 24, 1863.

19. Thomas, *Abraham Lincoln*, p. 459.

Chapter 7

1. CWAL, Vol. II, p. 438.

2. Ibid., p. 278.

3. Nicolay and Hay, *Abraham Lincoln*, Vol. IX, p. 40.

4. Adlai Ewing Stevenson, *Something of Men I Have Known*, p. 352. Told by Senator Henderson to Vice-President Stevenson.

5. John Wesley Hill, *Abraham Lincoln, Man of God* (1920), pp. 269-70.

6. CWAL, Vol. VII, p. 542. The Ostervald Bible of his parents which Lincoln used in the White House printed the following statement: "The Scriptures therefore are the most valuable blessing God ever bestowed upon us, except the sending his Son into the world; they are a treasure containing everything that can make us truly rich and truly happy."

7. L. E. Chittenden, *Recollections of President Lincoln and His Administration* (1891), pp. 448–50.

8. Carpenter, *Six Months at the White House*, p. 31.

9. Colonel Silas Burt, *Century Magazine*, February 1907. Reprinted in Rufus Wilson, *Lincoln among His Friends* (1942), p. 333.

10. Letter of Herndon to Weik, December 22, 1888.

11. Carl Sandburg, *The War Years* (1939), Vol. III, p. 369.

12. Reinhold Niebuhr, *Discerning the Signs of the Times* (1946), p. 131.

13. CWAL, Vol. IV, p. 274.

14. *Herndon's Life of Lincoln*, p. 67. Told to Herndon by his cousin.

15. Edgar DeWitt Jones, *Lincoln and the Preachers* (1948), p. 148.

16. Benjamin Thomas in Abraham Lincoln Association Papers, 1935.

Chapter 8

1. Carpenter, *Six Months at the White House*, p. 189.

2. CWAL, Vol. IV, p. 441.

3. James Wilson, *North American Review*, December 1896, p. 667.

4. CWAL, Vol. V, pp. 403–4.

5. James G. Randall, *Lincoln the President* (1945), Vol. II, p. 161.

6. Edmund Wilson, *Eight Essays* (1954), p. 189. In 1922, Nathaniel Stephenson wrote in his *Lincoln* (p. 267): "It was a lofty but grave religion that matured in his final stage. Was it due to far-away Puritan ancestors?"

7. II Samuel 7:10.

8. CWAL, Vol. IV, p. 220, and Vol. II, p. 89.

9. Ibid., Vol. IV, pp. 268, 270.

10. Ibid., Vol. III, p. 310.

11. Sidney Mead, "Abraham Lincoln's 'Last Best Hope of Earth': The American Dream of Destiny and Democracy," *Church History*, March 1954, p. 3. This is an excellent study.

12. CWAL, Vol. V, p. 478. There is an interesting account of this inter-

view in the Lincoln Papers, Library of Congress, under the date 1862, September (28).

13. CWAL, Vol. VII, p. 535. Mrs. Gurney's letters are in the Robert Todd Lincoln Collection in the Library of Congress.

14. Chittenden, *Recollections,* pp. 448ff.

15. CWAL, Vol. V, pp. 497–98.

16. Ibid., pp. 518–37. Annual Message to Congress, December 1862.

17. Ibid., Vol. VI, p. 30. The Final Proclamation of Emancipation.

Chapter 9

1. CWAL, Vol. VI, p. 64.

2. Ibid., pp. 155–56.

3. Ibid., p. 314.

4. Ibid., pp. 332.

5. Ibid., pp. 406–10. Letter to James C. Conkling.

6. Carpenter, *Six Months at the White House,* pp. 208–9.

7. CWAL, Vol. VI, pp. 496–97. First National Proclamation of Thanksgiving, 1863.

8. Roy P. Basler, *Abraham Lincoln, His Speeches and Writings* (1946), p. 42.

9. CWAL, Vol. VII, p. 23. This was the final text of the address that Lincoln sent to Alexander Bliss sometime after March 4, 1864, for the Baltimore Sanitary Fair.

Chapter 10

1. CWAL, Vol. VIII, p. 149. Annual Message, December 1864.

2. Thomas, *Abraham Lincoln,* p. 494.

3. CWAL, Vol. VII, pp. 281–83. Letter to Albert Hodges.

4. Ibid., Vol. VII, p. 368.

5. Ibid., Vol. VIII, pp. 55–56. Thanksgiving Proclamation of 1864.

6. Ibid., Vol. V, p. 343.

7. Ibid., p. 346.

8. Ibid., Vol. VIII, p. 101.

9. Ibid., Vol. VII, p. 302.

10. Ibid., Vol. VIII, pp. 332–33. Second Inaugural Address.

11. Ibid., p. 356. Letter to Thurlow Weed.

12. Reinhold Niebuhr, *The Irony of American History,* p. 172.

13. CWAL, Vol. VIII, p. 403. Italics added.

14. Ibid., p. 399.

15. Nathaniel Stephenson, *Lincoln* (1922), p. 264.

16. James Randall and Richard Current, *Lincoln the President* (1955), Vol. IV, pp. 375–77.

17. Whitney, *Life on the Circuit with Lincoln,* p. 246.

18. Isaac N. Arnold, *The Life of Abraham Lincoln* (1885), p. 446. Arnold's statement continued: "Belief in the existence of God, in the immortality of the soul, in the Bible as the revelation of God to man, in the efficacy and duty of prayer, in reverence toward the Almighty, and in love and charity to man, was the basis of his religion."

19. Noah Brooks's letter of December 31, 1872, to J. A. Reed.

20. This interpretation also finds some support in the statement of Dr. Gurley, Lincoln's Washington pastor: ". . . after the death of his son Willie, and his visit to the battlefield of Gettysburg, he said, with tears in his eyes, that he had lost confidence in everything but God, and that he now believed his heart was changed, and that he loved the Savior, and if he was not deceived in himself, it was his intention soon to make a profession of religion." (Quoted from Reed's lecture, p. 326, in Barton's Appendix.)

21. David C. Mearns, "Christian without a Creed," a printed address in the Library of Congress to the Young People of St. John's Church, February 13, 1955. Mearns's phrase is taken from a penciled note of Nicolay's: ". . . the world can utter no other verdict than this—He was a Christian without a creed"(p. 14).

22. Barton, *The Soul of Abraham Lincoln,* p. 289. The section in brackets is the writer's explanation of Baxter's meaning for the word "comfort."

Index